I0796855

The OBITUARY COCKTAIL

The Obituary Cocktail

SUE STRACHAN

LOUISIANA STATE UNIVERSITY PRESS
BATON ROUGE

Published by Louisiana State University Press
lsupress.org

Manufactured in the United States of America
First printing

Designer: Barbara Neely Bourgoyne
Typeface: Arno Pro
Printer and binder: Integrated Books International

Portions of chapter three were first published in the *Uptown Messenger* as "Endangered Places: French Benevolent Society Tomb in Lafayette Cemetery #2" (2021).

Cover photograph courtesy Ivy Withrow.

Frontispiece photo by Chris Granger (chrisgranger.com).

Cataloging-in-Publication Data are available from the Library of Congress.
ISBN 978-0-8071-8479-0 (cloth)

To my family, friends, bartenders, compatriots, coworkers, raconteurs, cocktailers, artists, characters, chroniclers, researchers, museums, bars, restaurants, and others who helped me create this homage to a legendary cocktail concocted in a legendary city, New Orleans.

CONTENTS

ACKNOWLEDGMENTS

I have to start by thanking Louisiana State University (LSU) Press and acquisitions editor Jenny Keegan for thinking of me to write this book. I guess the fun I had writing *The Café Brûlot,* which is also part of the LSU Press's Iconic New Orleans Cocktail series, persuaded them to offer me this new project! More thanks to production editor Ashley Gilly for her patience and keen eye for detail.

As with any book, there is a group of people who were important to the process. I'd first like to thank Neal Bodenheimer, cocktail guru and one of the busiest men in the city as he is managing partner of CureCo, which includes Cure (winner of a James Beard Award for "Outstanding Bar Program"), Cane & Table, and Vals in New Orleans; partner in Dauphine's in Washington, DC; and cochair of the board of directors for Tales of the Cocktail Foundation. Neal also is the coauthor of *Cure: New Orleans Drinks and How to Mix 'Em.* See what I mean about busy? But he was always there with enthusiasm, advice, and help with this book. Cure's Liz Kelley provided the Corpse Reviver recipe as well as organized the visuals for the cover image, among others. The fabulously talented Chris Granger was the photographer for those.

I am also very grateful for the contributions from local bars and restaurants: Fives and Columns owners Jayson Seidman and Garrison Neill with coordination by Kiley Laemmli and cocktail recipes by Fives' James O'Donnell and Columns' Eric Solis; Robert LeBlanc, founder and creative director of LeBlanc + Smith and its Barrel Proof, helmed by Liam Deegan; Dr. Benji Creel and his mother, Liz Creel, of the Gilded Perch in the ParkView Historic Hotel; Barkley Rafferty and Zach Hunt of Bar Epilogue, the Chicory House, as well as the Garden District Book shop's co-owner Carroll Gelderman Zimmer and its fabulous manager, Amy Loewy. More kudos to Jewel of the South's co-owner/head bartender Chris Hannah and general manager Paul Greagoff, as well as Delachaise Wine Bar & Bistro owner Evan Hayes. At Café Lafitte in Exile, owner Tom Wood and Beaux Church gave me some insight into that bar's history.

Thank you to Sazerac chairman Bill Goldring and Republic National Distributing's Fred Holley, who were on hand quickly to turn around an important question, as well as Sazerac archivist and exhibits director Nick Laracuente for the vintage Herbsaint images. Designer Phillip Collier, who has produced a number of informative books about New Orleans, also helped with images.

Not based in New Orleans but still important players in the cocktail scene (and this book), are Brown-Forman's Marshall Farrar and Simon Ford of Fords Gin, the latter of whom provided insightful input on the section about gin.

Fellow writers and journalists contributed in various and important ways. Frank Perez, a historian with a focus on gay history in New Orleans, was a great source and all-around fun to talk to. Jessica B. Harris, a renowned culinary historian, allowed me to use her recipe for the Zombie from her *Rum Drinks: 50 Caribbean Cocktails, from*

Cuba Libre to Rum Daisy. Bryan Dias of the *NOLADrinks Show* patiently answered my questions about vermouth. Also helpful were Marielle Songy, writer of *The Absinthe Frappé,* which is part of the LSU Iconic New Orleans Cocktail series; and Ted Breaux, an absinthe expert, consultant, and coauthor of *Absinthe: The Exquisite Elixir,* as well as the distiller/owner of the Jade absinthes, and creator/ambassador of Lucid Absinthe, owned by Hood River Distillers.

I met Jim Marshall Wilson and his husband, Adam Hostetter, at an absinthe event that Marielle Songy and Ted Breaux did at the Southern Food and Beverage (SoFAB) Museum, which also houses the Museum of the American Cocktail. Wilson's mother was a cousin of Roger "Tom" Caplinger, co-owner of Café Lafitte, where the Obituary Cocktail was created, and he'd donated some of her ephemera to the Historic New Orleans Collection (HNOC)—thank you to the HNOC team of Heather Green and Rebecca Smith for sourcing those in the collection. Wilson also provided some early leads to researching the history of Café Lafitte, now Café Lafitte in Exile.

One of the fun things to discover was the Grande and Secret Order of Obituary Cocktail, a cocktail-loving group that meets on Friday evenings at different bars in New Orleans. The group's Arlene Karcher was a great help with unlocking the "secrets," including those from founder Dorian Bennett and artist Freddie Guess, who did a wonderful painting of the group in its early years. The group was inspired by the book *Obituary Cocktail: The Great Saloons of New Orleans,* by Kerri McCaffety, a beautiful homage to the great bars of New Orleans.

More kudos to Tony Leggio and Rene Fransen, who helped me track down a source; Bradley Sumrall, who loaned me a rare copy of the book *The Bachelor in New Orleans,* which offers an interesting peek into French Quarter life in the early 1940s; and artist Mitchell Gaudet, who is also knowledgeable about death traditions in New Orleans and provided insight about that subject.

I did my own mini writer's retreat in Waveland and Bay St. Louis, Mississippi (as I did with my previous book, *The Café Brûlot*), so thank you again, Jena Regan, whose cottage was the perfect place to do the last push for the book, and our mutual friend Susan Boyd Bright for introducing us. If you are in Bay St. Louis, don't forget to stop in at Mockingbird Cafe, one of my favorite places to work (and eat).

Kudos to Dustin Blitchok, whose enthusiasm about this book was greatly appreciated, and to Andrew Nelson, fellow writer and traveler, who, when I was having a writer's block, would always cajole me out of it.

Thank you to my late Aunt Janet and Uncle Tom Doody for lagniappe, Aunt Cathie Upp for being a fan, and finally to my mother, Doris Strachan, who always diligently asked me how the book was going—no pressure, honestly, but kept me on my toes, as a good mother should.

Opposite: The finishing touch on an Obituary Cocktail at Cure. Photo by Chris Granger.

The OBITUARY COCKTAIL

Bottles of ingredients for the Obituary Cocktail made by Cure. Photo by Chris Granger.

INTRODUCTION

> First you take a drink, then the drink takes
> a drink, then the drink takes you.
>
> —F. SCOTT FITZGERALD

There are few cocktails that pique more interest among friends, coworkers, strangers, and other boisterous sorts than the Obituary Cocktail. First—and the obvious place to start—is the name. What could actually be in a drink named for what is essentially a death notice? What drink could be so potent it deserves such an intriguing and somewhat ominously creative name? This one.

A combination of gin, vermouth, and absinthe, the Obituary Cocktail starts off strong—the first taste, depending on how it is concocted, can make it seem as if the drink is all absinthe, which has a heavy anise (think licorice) flavor. For some, it tastes like mouthwash.

But don't give up on it. Upon the second sip, once the palate has adjusted, the gin, vermouth, and absinthe—strong liquors that, depending on the style, can have bold flavors—blend together for a drink that is smooth, sophisticated, clarifying, ultimately pleasing—and intoxicating. It is a cocktail that could make you ponder—or tell—your life's story or possibly give you a good night's sleep.

While the cocktail has been gaining a place in many a bar program menu in New Orleans and across the U.S., it also owes the familiarity of its name to the book *Obituary Cocktail: The Great Saloons of New Orleans,* a beautiful tome by Kerri McCaffety published in 1998. McCaffety photographed a number of the city's bars, most still in existence, a few sadly closed. The book includes Lafitte's Blacksmith Shop, the structure (still an operating bar) where Café Lafitte was located when the Obituary Cocktail was created, before it moved down the street in 1953 to become Café Lafitte in Exile. Also known today as Lafitte's (a shorter version of the formal name), it is considered the oldest continuously open gay bar in the U.S.

McCaffety approaches these bars in a joyful and reverent manner, not one of sorrow or melancholy. It's fitting for a city that celebrates death differently than anywhere else in the U.S.: jazz funerals with second lines, All Saints' Day, and Día de Muertos (Day of the Dead).

New Orleans is where the past is present, the present is past, which is very much in the spirit of the Obituary Cocktail—and this book.

The following are four recipes for the Obituary Cocktail, each with a distinct difference, but all delicious. Enjoy!

OBITUARY COCKTAIL

SERVES 1

Courtesy Beaux Church, Café Lafitte in Exile

2 ounces Woody Creek Gin

1 ounce Cinzano Vermouth

1 ounce Copper & Kings Absinthe Alembic

Combine all of the ingredients in a mixing glass, stir with ice, then pour into a glass.

ABOUT CAFÉ LAFITTE IN EXILE: The bar where the Obituary Cocktail was invented, Café Lafitte in Exile continues the tradition of serving it. Manager Beaux Church says he likes the Colorado-based distiller Woody Creek gin because it has more juniper and less floral flavor to it. (For more in-depth history about the bar, go to chapter 1.)

OBITUARY COCKTAIL

SERVES 1

Courtesy Neal Bodenheimer, Cure

1½ ounces Plymouth Navy Strength Gin

¾ ounce Noilly Prat Original Dry Vermouth

¾ ounce Dolin Dry Vermouth

1 dash Bittercube Orange Bitters

Vieux Pontarlier Absinthe

Combine all ingredients listed above, except absinthe, with ice and stir until chilled. Season a chilled cocktail glass with seven sprays of absinthe from an atomizer. Strain liquids into the absinthe-seasoned glass. Express a lemon peel over the drink and discard the peel.

ABOUT CURE: Cure was opened in 2009 in New Orleans by Neal Bodenheimer, Matthew Kohnke, and Kirk Estopinal. It quickly became the place to be seen and a scene for cocktails, and it is largely credited for pioneering the modern-day craft cocktail movement in New Orleans. The bar/restaurant was recognized for its efforts by being named the 2018 winner of the James Beard Award for "Outstanding Bar Program," one of "American's Best Bars" by *Esquire,* and listed as one of the "Best Cocktail Bars in the U.S." by *Food & Wine.*

OBITUARY COCKTAIL

SERVES 1

Courtesy James O'Donnell, Fives

2¼ ounces Sipsmith London Dry Gin

¾ ounce La Quintinye Dry Vermouth

5–6 dashes Jade Nouvelle-Orléans Absinthe

Lemon twist

Combine the first three ingredients in a mixing glass. Add ice to about halfway, stir well, then strain into a chilled coupe. Garnish with a lemon twist. [Note: It is important to add the ice after the liquor to get the correct dilution.]

When James O'Donnell makes this drink, he likes an additional spritz of absinthe over the top of the finished cocktail. He loves the richness and intensity of flavor from the La Quintinye Dry Vermouth because it can stand up to the addition of absinthe.

Jade Nouvelle-Orléans Absinthe, O'Donnell noted, was created by a native New Orleanian, Ted Breaux. "Its history is deeply rooted in our city. It only made sense to reach for this bottle when making a recipe first popularized at [Café Lafitte at] Lafitte's Blacksmith Shop," he said.

ABOUT FIVES: Fives opened in 2023 in New Orleans, located in the Lower Pontalba Building, opening out to the French Quarter's Jackson Square. It is known for its craft cocktails and raw bar, including oysters and other seafood, caviar, among other offerings.

OBITUARY COCKTAIL

SERVES 1

Courtesy Chris Hannah, Jewel of the South

2 ounces Fords London Dry Gin

¾ ounce Dolin Dry Vermouth

¼ ounce absinthe

1 bar spoon green crème de menthe

Lemon twist

Olive

Combine all ingredients except olive and lemon twist in a mixing glass and stir. Pour into a chilled cocktail glass. Finish the with an olive and a lemon twist placed on a cocktail pick.

ABOUT JEWEL OF THE SOUTH: Jewel of the South is a restaurant and bar nestled in an early nineteenth-century Creole cottage in the French Quarter. Since it opened in March 2019, its cocktail program, led by co-owner and award-winning head bartender Chris Hannah, has made fans around the world and was named as one of "North America's 50 Best Bars" on the annual list published by William Reed.

NOTE: A variation not in these recipes, but which I enjoyed at The Ordinary in Charleston, South Carolina, is to use an 80/20 saline solution instead of vermouth.

THE GRANDE AND SECRET ORDER OF OBITUARY COCKTAIL

It's Friday night in New Orleans, and a sizable group of people have gathered at a local watering hole. Not an unusual occurrence, of course, but for this night and bar, it was special because the establishment was chosen for fun, frivolity, and cocktails by the Grande and Secret Order of Obituary Cocktail.

Who is in this mysterious group? Its creation was inspired by Kerri McCaffety's *Obituary Cocktail: The Great Saloons of New Orleans,* which documented the city's bars. When the book was published in 1998, it spurred a renewed interest in these establishments, as well as cocktails. This included the Obituary Cocktail, which faded from memory during the late twentieth and early twenty-first centuries except in the select local places that made it—as well as among those in the know.

The book definitely made an impression on art collector and real estate broker Dorian Bennett, who, after getting the book as a birthday gift, decided to bring it to a dinner party at the French Quarter home of his friend Mathilde Leary—he says most likely in 1999—to show friends. "I walked over to the party and introduced the book to all of these characters who were preservationists from different parts of town," said Bennett. "They hadn't heard of the book yet. I asked them if they had been to these bars and they said they had not." Bennett then issued a challenge to the crowd to visit all of the featured bars. And with that, the Grande and Secret Order of Obituary Cocktail was born. In addition to using the book title/cocktail, the name was a clever nod to the city's "secret" societies.

The first bar the friends visited was the Napoleon House, followed by others in the French Quarter. "We would bring our books with us to each of the bars and we would autograph them like it was a yearbook," said Bennett. The group has now expanded to bars elsewhere in the city. And, while members may come and go, the gatherings always take place on a Friday, usually between 6:00 and 7:00 p.m.

There is no organizational structure; as the group's biography boasts, "Then do not expect any efficiency, organization, governing boards, structure, bylaws, organizational meetings, budget, elections, goals, objectives, required attendance rules or a responsible leader or even a leader, because none of those exist."

There have been gatherings featuring as few as twenty, and at others there have been more than one hundred, said the society, adding that some people have tried to predict how many people will be at different locations. The group also took their gatherings on the road by traveling by private bus to bars in neighboring areas, and others have gone to San Miguel de Allende, Mexico. From book to dinner party to bars—who wouldn't want to join a group that celebrates cocktails and conviviality in New Orleans? (And the Obituary Cocktail, too.)

Opposite: Block-print ad for Café Lafitte in *The Bachelor in New Orleans: A Handbook for Unattached Gentlemen and Ladies of Spirit Visiting or Resident in the Paris of America* [1942], by Robert Kinney, with illustrations by Eugenia and Bob Riley. The Historic New Orleans Collection, 78-322-RL.

941 BOURBON
Café Lafitte
Nouvelle Orleans
whatever the hour
there's always fun at
CAFE LAFITTE

CHAPTER ONE

DEATH BECOMES A DRINK

THE ORIGINS OF THE OBITUARY COCKTAIL

Sometimes too much to drink is barely enough.

—MARK TWAIN

The birth of the Obituary Cocktail, like most New Orleans cocktails and tales, starts in the city's French Quarter. The French Quarter in the 1940s, when the Obituary Cocktail was said to be invented, was redolent of sex, secrets, and excitement. It was the place your parents told you was dangerous, which of course made it even more alluring.

Anything could happen among the narrow streets flanked by architecture of bygone eras in varying states of decay, some still highlighted by cast-iron balconies, or along the neon-filled Bourbon Street of burlesque and nightclubs. Reflecting the city's prominence as a port, wharves lined the Mississippi River, limiting access to it. Prostitution lingered despite nearby Storyville being closed since 1917. Bohemian culture flourished, and, in other parts, the backdrop was immigrants from all over, including Sicily, Italy, and China. The city overall was segregated. The French Quarter was the setting of Tennessee Williams's *A Streetcar Named Desire,* but it also attracted high society, as portrayed in *Dinner at Antoine's* by Frances Parkinson Keyes.

The French Quarter is the oldest part of the New Orleans, founded in 1718 by Jean-Baptiste Le Moyne de Bienville. This adventurer and statesman is often depicted as bewigged and in the formal attire befitting an eighteenth-century gentleman, but unseen beneath his finery, his body was covered in snake tattoos, which he got from Native Americans. Bienville set the tone for New Orleans: what one sees on the formal surface often hides a more seductive reality. And it was the only milieu where the Obituary Cocktail could be concocted.

But first, a little history.

The Volstead Act, aka Prohibition, which started in 1920, had just been lifted on December 5, 1933. While New Orleans had played somewhat fast and loose with banning alcohol and drinking, the relief was no doubt palpable that one could now have a beer, a glass of wine, or a cocktail in public.

Enter Roger "Tom" Caplinger, Harold Barthel, and Mary Collins, who in 1933 leased a building at 941 Bourbon Street, at the corner of St. Philip Street, opening a bar named Café Lafitte. Barthel made regular appearances in the newspapers of 1920s and 1930s, attending society parties, including debutante fêtes and Carnival events; some newspaper columnists called him a socialite. Collins had a fondness for cats and Scotch, was gay, and dressed in men's clothing (not necessarily the norm during the 1930s). Most

Lafitte's Blacksmith Shop, ca. 1945–1955, by Homer Emory Turner. The Historic New Orleans Collection, gift of Ms. Beverly T. Lynds, 2002.84.66.

articles about the bar during that time focused on Caplinger, a raconteur, actor, bon vivant—and the Blue Book 1954 winner as the "The Quarter's Best-Dressed Man." In addition to co-owning the bar, Caplinger was married to Marion (née Zabriskie) and had four children—Dorothy Lane Caplinger, William Caplinger, John Caplinger, and one who went on to become renowned actress Grace Zabriskie, who had roles in *Twin Peaks, Seinfeld, Norma*

Rae, and *The Grudge.* The bar became popular among French Quarter bohemians, artists, writers; it was also as "gay-friendly" as the era would allow.

OBITUARY COCKTAIL'S DEBUT

In 1942, *The Bachelor in New Orleans* by Robert Kinney was published, a rapturous tome about the city's bars, restaurants, and other distractions, as well as tips on how to be a good tourist. The book bills itself as "A handbook for unattached gentlemen and ladies of spirit visiting or resident in the Paris of America," adding that it is also "a handbook for those not afraid to find out for themselves." A little ominous, but cocktailing in New Orleans has never been for amateurs.

Of cocktails in the city, Kinney writes, "That drinks exist in New Orleans, drinks that never taste the same anywhere else, is not merely a rumor. Wondrous drinks there are, and in great quantity."

It's good to know things haven't changed since then.

Of Café Lafitte, Kinney declares, "An atmosphere of complete informality prevails here: if the bartender is passed out, go behind the bar and mix your own!"

The Obituary Cocktail is mentioned, showing up in good company early in the book, when Kinney writes about local specialties, including a Ramos Gin Fizz, Absinthe Frappé, and Café Brûlot. Kinney interestingly mentions a New Orleans Martini, which is "made with Louisiana orange wine in place of vermouth."

Kinney wrote that two drinks were exclusive to Café Lafitte: the Obituary Cocktail and the Lafitte Special, which, according to the book, contains applejack, curaçao, and other ingredients. If you are lucky enough to see—or even purchase—an original copy of the book, the block prints by Eugenia and Bob Riley are also entertaining. The images of restaurants and bars are sometimes mysterious and often quite witty.

So now we know the drink was around in the early 1940s at Café Lafitte. Its subsequent presence and fame were then cemented by its periodic appearance in the local newspapers. "New Orleans' latest drink, incidentally, is a cocktail called Obituary, invented by Tom Caplinger, owner of Jean Lafitte's bar [*sic*] (add a drop of absinthe to a Manhattan or a Martini and it becomes an Obituary)," wrote Danton Walker, a columnist known for his musings about nightlife and the city, in the June 16, 1948, *New Orleans Item.*

Thomas Griffin, another nightlife columnist for the *New Orleans Item* and the author of *The Pelican Guide to New Orleans: Touring America's Most Interesting City,* wrote in his "Lagniappe" column of April 13, 1950, "to Cafe Lafitte after . . . sign on table: 'Try an Obituary cocktail' . . . Tom Caplinger swearing 'Obituary' is purely coincidental to present activity in the Quarter . . . drink has Ojen (the Spanish absynthe) in it, says he."

The use of anise-flavored Ojen, produced in Spain, is interesting, but it is not absinthe. It was a popular liqueur in New Orleans and was used in the Ojen cocktail—a mixture of Ojen, Peychaud's bitters, and simple syrup with a lemon twist—which was the preferred drink of the city's blue bloods during Carnival, and in particular with members of the Rex organization.

The Ojen substitution for absinthe brings up the question, What else did Café Lafitte use if absinthe was still banned in the U.S.? Absinthe was not allowed in the U.S. from 1912 to 2007, but it's not a stretch to assume there were bottles of absinthe floating around the city, whether a secret stash or "smuggled" in.

There is also the curious case of the Jitters cocktail, a recipe of which was said to have first appeared on the back of bottles of Fernandez White Label Ojen, produced in Spain. In 1937, the recipe also popped up in *Famous New Orleans Drinks and How to Mix 'Em,* by Stanley Clisby Arthur. "Barkeepers who claim that Ojen should not be mixed with other liquors, say this one ought to give anybody the 'jitters,'" he wrote, divulging the recipe of "⅓ jigger Ojen, ⅓ jigger gin and ⅓ jigger French vermouth."

Was the Jitters an inspiration for the Obituary Cocktail? Or was the Ojen a matter of practicality: a Café Lafitte bartender or one of the owners ran out of absinthe (if they had it) or even Herbsaint, with Ojen the only thing on hand to make the concoction?

And, let's talk about Herbsaint, which was created in New Orleans and wasn't sold until 1934, post-Prohibition.

One difference between absinthe and Herbsaint is that Herbsaint does not contain grand wormwood, which has the chemical thujone, once believed to be responsible for the hallucinations and other issues often associated with absinthe. Herbsaint is an anise-flavored liqueur, and it would have been a good substitute: it is sometimes used today in the Obituary Cocktail and for other cocktails that call for absinthe.

Perhaps, one day, we may find out exactly the Obituary Cocktail's New Orleans origin story, but as with most tales of the city, it remains a mystery with a few diverting story-lines.

CAFÉ LAFITTE, PART 1 (BEFORE THE EXILE: LAFITTE BROTHERS)

No story about the invention of the Obituary Cocktail is complete without a history of Café Lafitte, now known as Café Lafitte in Exile (though often shortened to Lafitte's), and Lafitte's Blacksmith Shop.

Lafitte's Blacksmith Shop, called *Spanish House,* ca. 1883–1886, in a stereograph by George François Mugnier. The Historic New Orleans Collection, 1999.98.2.

Even though Café Lafitte and Lafitte's Blacksmith Shop have not been linked since 1953—when Café Lafitte moved and became Café Lafitte in Exile, more on that later—they are sometimes treated as one and the same.

In *New Orleans Drinks and How to Mix Them,* by Jack D. L. Holmes, the author was seemingly unaware of the connection between Lafitte's Blacksmith Shop and Café Lafitte in Exile, writing in 1973, "Once located at 941 Bourbon, alas this tavern is no more. The specialty of the house used to be a dry martini with a lingering taste of absinthe, which they called the Obituary. Apparently, the Obituary brought the death of the establishment." It's a clever turn of phrase but not good history: Café Lafitte in Exile and Lafitte's Blacksmith Shop were both in business at that time.

So let's start at the beginning with privateer and smuggler Jean Lafitte and Lafitte's Blacksmith Shop. Both have origin stories that evolve and change through the years, so separating fact from fiction can be daunting—and will remain so.

The first myth to bust is that Jean Lafitte and his brother Pierre Lafitte were the ones who built the structure at 941

Bourbon Street. The problem is that of timing. Looking at the Collins C. Diboll Vieux Carré Digital Survey, Lot no. 319 was granted on January 1, 1722, to Jean Cossine and Nicolas Touze. (The digital survey references historical, architectural, legal, and sociological data on individual lots and structures from the French Colonial period.)

Though some sources say Touze had the house built, subsequent property transfers—in 1728, 1731, 1761 and 1773—do not indicate a house on the lot. That said, the Gornichon Map from 1731 shows a small structure (and a different street number, but the blocks line up), and it is hard to say whether the building is the one there today or whether the original building was a casualty of the fires of 1788 or 1794.

The Duroche Castillon House, as it is known in preservation circles, is thought to have been constructed sometime between 1770 and the 1790s. The city was then under Spanish rule (1762–1803). One source cites 1772 as the date, and a property transfer in 1781 states there was a building on the lot, but another source notes it was built most likely around 1795 (after both of the city's fires). It was built in *colombage* and *brique-entre-poteaux* in a French Colonial, though some say Norman, cottage style. The original overhanging roof was eliminated, and dormers were added over time.

In 1781, Bartholome Robert, who owned the property, gave it to his daughter Marguerite Robert Duroche and her husband, Simon Duroche, who, according to a source, was a castellan, which would have meant he was in charge of the city's fortifications. Mrs. Duroche owned it until 1833, when it appears she gave it to her daughter, Manette Duroche St. Germain.

Jean Lafitte was nowhere near the scene in mid- to late eighteenth-century New Orleans—nor could he have been—when the building was constructed. Lafitte was born to Pierre Lafitte [Sr.] and Marguerite Desteil (Lafitte's second wife) circa 1780, some say in Pauillac, near the Bordeaux region of France, whereas others place his birth in the French colony of Saint-Domingue (now Haiti).

Even Jean's arrival in the U.S. is murky. He either arrived with his mother and older brother Pierre (the child of the first wife and Pierre Sr., who was deceased at this point), or Pierre arrived in 1803 among refugees seeking asylum from the Haitian Revolution, with Jean following sometime in 1804.

The year 1803 is pivotal in New Orleans history. That was when France sold 828,000 square miles of land west of the Mississippi River for $15 million to the U.S., doubling the nation's size. The deal is most famously known as the Louisiana Purchase.

New Orleans was dominated by Creoles, free people of color, Native Americans, Spanish, and French. It was a major port of legal and illegal goods. Pierre was already engaged in the slave trade in some aspect as a merchant when Jean arrived. By 1809, Jean was known as "the notorious Captain Lafitte," probably due to his work as a privateer. Though legend said Pierre used 941 Bourbon Street as a front, acting as a blacksmith, some sources say he wasn't a blacksmith, while others say brothers were working out of a warehouse on Royal Street. The rumor of the Lafitte brothers as blacksmiths seems to have popped up in the fictional "Madame Delphine" by George Washington Cable, published 1881. The story has been carried on through the years, but thus far no records confirm them as blacksmiths or the building being used as a blacksmith shop. What is known as fact is that Pierre and Jean Lafitte went to help American forces against the British during the War of 1812 and are often credited for providing critical support during the Battle of New Orleans in 1815, adding to legend.

We'll probably never know for sure exactly what was going on at 941 Bourbon Street while the Lafitte brothers were doing illicit business in the city, but the legend of their connection to it lives on at Lafitte's Blacksmith Shop, a bar famous for this history and its "Voodoo Daiquiri," aka "the purple drink," aka "purple drank"—and as the location where the Obituary Cocktail was created.

CAFÉ LAFITTE, PART 2: (BEFORE THE EXILE: MIDCENTURY BONHOMIE)

When Café Lafitte opened its doors in 1933, the three partners, Barthel, Collins, and Caplinger, were riding the post-Prohibition wave; New Orleans was a city ready to party—

even more. Café Lafitte was a hit with the city's bohemian crowd—one could argue the three owners were already part of it—as well as the Uptown (society) set, most likely attracted to it for its sophisticated but risqué ambiance and Barthel, who was part of that milieu.

"It was a gathering place for the late-night artsy crowd. The most attractive people in the world talking about the most interesting things," said Ella Brennan, according to a *Times-Picayune* article. Brennan, who most know from Commander's Palace fame, was working with her older brother Owen Brennan, most likely in the late 1940s/early 1950s, when he owned the Vieux Carré restaurant. She also fondly remembered Café Lafitte, saying (with a few variations), "Most girls went to finishing school, I went to Café Lafitte." Another local restaurant notable would also pop in: Count Arnaud Cazenave of Arnaud's restaurant. Cazenave, though he was born in France, really wasn't a count; he just called himself one.

The bar also attracted visitors from around the U.S. and world. "Before the jet plane, there was no jet set, darlin'—there was Café Lafitte . . . Everybody was there," said Ella

Tennessee Williams and Pancho Rodriguez at Café Lafitte, 1946. The Historic New Orleans Collection, gift of James M. Wilson in memory of Violet Gwendolyn Dieterich Wilson, 2023.0080.4.

Brennan in a *New York Times* article. That also included politicians, with Brennan noting that Louisiana politicians Earl Long and Chep Morrison could be seen there, along with national figures Herbert Humphrey and Eugene McCarthy, both of whom went on to run unsuccessfully for president.

Artist Enrique Alférez, whose sculptures have a dedicated sculpture garden today in New Orleans City Park, was a loyal fan of the bar and created the *Adam and Eve* (also known as *The Lovers*) sculpture, which is still in the courtyard of Lafitte's Blacksmith Shop.

The bar was also a haven for a gay clientele, including authors like Gore Vidal, Truman Capote, and Lyle Saxon, who was part of the French Quarter's "Dixie Bohemia" heyday of the 1920s and was essential to the area's early twentieth-century preservation efforts. Playwright Tennessee Williams was a familiar face who, it was said, among other things, enjoyed the piano playing of "Miss Lily" Hood.

It's significant that Café Lafitte was gay-friendly—and today (as Café Lafitte in Exile) it is considered the oldest continuously open gay bar in the U.S. But at that time, there was a city ordinance prohibiting bar owners from serving "degenerates." Bars that did so could be raided by the police, so the co-owners of Café Lafitte were at risk.

Despite that, Café Lafitte's doors were open, and its ambiance was well publicized, with newspaper columnists writing frequently "tongue-in-cheek" about the bar. In his February 1949 *New Orleans Item* "Lagniappe" column, Thomas Griffin wrote, "To Cafe Lafitte afterward" . . . Host Tom Caplinger showed me an article by Lucius Beebe in the February 'Gourmet' which plugs the New Orleans Mardi Gras as the wildest celebration of any he's witnessed . . . and describes the Cafe Lafitte as a 'gaudy el dump' which looks like a haunted farmhouse on the outside, and inside resembles nothing so much as 'Halloween in Hell.'" Griffin adds, "the proprietors would be alarmed if you described it any other way." And couples were married at Café Lafitte: "Tom Caplinger just helped his 54th couple tie the knot that binds," reported a May 1946 article in the *New Orleans Item.*

At one point, the bar branched out: Griffin reported in an August 1949 *New Orleans Item* article that the Café

Lafitte was "opening an 'uptown' branch a few blocks further up the street tonight with socialite Harold Barthel in charge; they're going to call it Cafe Lafitte, Uptown." The affiliate location was in the backstage area of nightclub Dan's International, situated at 600 Bourbon Street, at the corner of Toulouse Street. Today the building is home to Tropical Isle. As Barthel was known for his piano-playing skills at the original, he put them to good use here too. At some point, Café Lafitte, Uptown, closed.

Barthel and Collins sold their interest in Café Lafitte in 1951 to Lee Smith. The duo went on to found the Galley House, which opened in 1957. Like Café Lafitte and its "Uptown" version, this bar was a popular hangout: "This charming bistro . . . caters to the literati and the more avante avante garde. Patrons at the Galley House, Chartres and Toulouse, provide much of their own music and singing and at times, bedlam is said to reign," said the *New Orleans Item* "Where to Go" column in 1958. Eventually, the Galley House became known as the "Wrinkle Room" due to the age of its clientele. But we're getting ahead of the Exile part of the story.

941
RUE
BOURBON
NOUVELLE
ORLEANS

CARTE POSTALE

CORRESPONDANCE

ADRESSE

NEW ORLEANS
MAR 25
7:30 PM
1947
LA.

UNITED STATES
1 CENT 1

Dear Cousin
Ollie – thanks for
your note – have told
Mother + Dady. We
all feel badly, though
Mrs Shipley had told
them about Cousin Grace.
We enjoyed having
the girls with us.
Love Roger.

Mrs C. P. Dietrich
Maysville
Ky.

6B-H429

2023.0080.39

Café Lafitte at Lafitte's Blacksmith Shop. Postcard from Roger [Tom] Caplinger to Mrs. C. P. [Dieterich] Wilson, 1947. The Historic New Orleans Collection, gift of James M. Wilson in memory of Violet Gwendolyn Dieterich Wilson, 2023.0080.39.

CAFÉ LAFITTE, PART 3: (THE EXILE AND TODAY)

Caplinger, Collins, and Barthel created a place where everyone felt comfortable being themselves. Their generosity also extended to showcasing art for sale on the walls without taking a commission, and setting up tabs for patrons, which were usually not paid. This would come back to haunt Caplinger.

In 1953, the owner of the building, John Barbe, died. The title was unclear, so per court order it had to go to auction. When the auction was announced, Caplinger assured the interiors were not for sale. Griffin noted, "Fifteen years ago, when Tom Caplinger first saw it for [sale? word missing] the tag was $5,500." It was, alas, no longer so inexpensive.

The auction on February 4, 1953, was in the bar's patio, spilling inside, and, according to the *New Orleans Item,* was attended by Caplinger, the bar's former patrons and supporters, such as author Bob Tallant, restaurateur Owen Brennan, and "a covey of debutantes from this year, last year, and 10, 20 and 30 years ago; a smattering of confused tourists; 'Ricque [Enrique] Alférez . . . Some serious-looking men in business suits and some unserious-ones in polo shirts." Also on hand was Alonzo Lansford, director of the Delgado Art Museum (now the New Orleans Museum of Art), who hoped to bid on the Alférez sculpture, though it wasn't part of the auction.

Griffin, in his *New Orleans Item* column, described the crowd as "characters from all stratas of cafe society." Those bidding included "Omer Claiborne, Virginia Helis, Dottie Reiger, French Quarter bar owner [Joe] Joseph and a heavy set stranger in dark glasses." (Claiborne's sister was renowned fashion designer Liz Claiborne. They were descendants of William C. C. Claiborne, Louisiana's first governor, 1812–16.)

Led by auctioneer Sam Goldberg, bids started, going up in one-hundred-dollar increments. The Claiborne-Helis faction stood "under the patio's fig tree," while Caplinger stayed inside with former manager Tony Devine, who claimed he had a certified check for forty thousand dollars from a Bay St. Louis bank and was representing the Rockefeller and Guggenheim foundations. He was allegedly going to "tear the cafe down and build an ice skating rink as the St. Moritz of North America."

The first bid of $5,000 came from "Bouffie" Claiborne and Omer, who were "the principal backers of Caplinger," and at some point earlier had bought an interest in the bar, possibly buying out Lee Smith. The bidding continued, up to $17,500, and the Claibornes and "a stranger" bid it up to $30,000. Joe Joseph, who owned Tony Bacino's bar, which welcomed a gay clientele, entered the bidding war, topping the bid. Dottie Rieger, who told Griffin she was bidding for a client, kicked it up to $40,000, and the Claibornes dropped out. At this point, Virginia Helis, whose family was in oil, jumped into the bidding, intending "to retain Caplinger as cafe maestro."

It went up to $42,000, with Helis and Joseph in a bidding war, and when it reached $42,500, Helis and the Claibornes discussed, according to Griffin, going to $50,000. Caplinger told his friends to stop as he surmised that the competition was going to top any subsequent bid. Joseph won with a $42,500 bid.

"Joseph announced briefly that he intended to run the cafe in its established manner," in the *New Orleans Item* article. The "established manner" ultimately did not include Caplinger. Griffin wrote the day of the auction, "The new owner, 'Joe' Joseph, says he has [illegible] immediate plans for changing the place . . . 'After all,' he said, 'Caplinger has 30 more days [in] which to vacate. After that, I see no reason [illegible] an establishment that's making [money?, partially obscured].'" Interestingly, Griffin also wrote that Joseph said he bought the place for himself and wasn't fronting for anybody. Years later, a box was found with all the outstanding bar tabs, which, when totaled, would have allowed Caplinger to buy the bar.

Caplinger and Barthel signed a lease on a building at the other end of the same block—it appears that Collins returned to help run the place about a year later—with the new name of Café Lafitte in Exile at 901 Bourbon Street.

On Café Lafitte's last day at 941 Bourbon Street, Caplinger brought a coffin to the café's patio. He got into the coffin and refused to come out. Then, his daughter Grace Zabriskie said in an interview, one of the waiters "called my mother and she came over with what she says was the only souffle she ever made that really rose properly." Zabriskie said her father then got out of the coffin and ate the souffle. Also, on the day of the move in late March 1953, Caplinger, "the irrepressible 'evictee,'" wrote Griffin, "tossed a 'Displaced Persons' party at his Cafe Lafitte in Exile the other p.m.; most guests came as refugees from his old joint."

Legend has it that in this grand opening party, some of the regulars, dressed as their favorite exile, started at the old location at 941 Bourbon Street, had a few drinks, then stood up, grabbed their bar stools, and marched them to 901 Bourbon Street. Zabriskie said that her father told everyone to dress in burlap sacks. That night, to avoid being raided, the front door was barricaded with sandbags and barbed wire, forcing people go to the back door to get in. It appears that it remained that way for a while.

Over at Lafitte's Blacksmith Shop, in June 1953, new owner Joe Joseph and management team Tony Bacino and Tony Devine had a party to mark the "reopening" of Lafitte's Blacksmith Shop. Devine, according to Griffin's *New Orleans Item* column, tried to shoe a horse but finally asked a J. E. Collins, "the blacksmith in residence," to finish the job. Well-wishers "poured" in and expressed "approval of the few changes for the better (a new bar, some paneling along the walls, a new brick wall in the patio)." Among these guests was author Robert Tallant.

Joseph sold the building in 1958, according to the Vieux Carré Digital Survey, to a corporation named Lafitte's Blacksmith Shop, Inc., which, according to Louisiana Secretary of State business filings, still owns it.

Café Lafitte in Exile's building at 901 Bourbon Street had a very unsteady-looking awning, no balcony, and no stucco. A photo, most likely from the 1950s or so, also shows that the windows facing Bourbon Street were shut. This was to ensure that passersby couldn't see the bar's patrons. Artist Enrique Alférez was said to have designed the bar. He did design a fountain where the "eternal flame" endures. The fountain is no longer in operation but often serves as a place for patrons to put their drinks.

Caplinger, Barthel, and Collins continued with what they did best at their former location: provide good drinks, entertainment, and a safe space (as much as it could be for the times) for gays. Tennessee Williams and Truman Capote moved their business over there, as did other patrons from 941 Bourbon Street—one story says that eventually the management at Lafitte's Blacksmith Shop did not want gays there.

Sadly, Caplinger only held court at Café Lafitte in Exile for about three years. He was found dead on March 26, 1956, by the bar's porter, Fred Martin, in a cot located in the back of the bar where Caplinger often would sleep when he worked late. Caplinger was fifty years old, dying on his sixteenth wedding anniversary. Ownership of the bar passed sometime in the late 1950s, possibly early 1960s, to Tommy Hopkins, who lived upstairs and was known to be straight.

Up until the late 1960s, the bar was known as a place where men would bring their female dates, then return later in the night and "meet who you really wanted to meet," said Tom Wood, the current owner of Café Lafitte in Exile. Though there were some exceptions, the bar eventually was not welcoming to Black or female patrons up until the 1990s.

In 1969, the building got an unintended "makeover."

35mm slide of image of Café Lafitte in Exile, ca. 1970s, by anonymous photographer. Collection of Anderson-Wallis Family.

The son of a diplomat had a fight with his lover in the bar and was asked to leave by the staff. He stormed out of the bar, got in his pickup truck parked across the street, and drove through the front of the bar, ripping off twenty feet of the Bourbon Street facade. Once Hopkins had the insurance money in hand, he had the building covered with stucco and added the balcony with help from architect

Leon Impastato. They converted the second-floor apartment into a restaurant, which only lasted a brief time.

When Hopkins sold the bar in 1975, he kept one of the paintings on the wall. The bar was once known for showing artists' work for sale, and one, nicknamed *Mother,* of a woman baring her breast, never sold. A copy was made of it, but it is unclear if Hopkins kept the original, or if it's the one that remains in the bar today.

According to Café Lafitte in Exile lore, Hopkins sold the bar to Ben Brown and Tom Wood, and by 1978, Wood solely owned it. Wood fixed it up in the early 1980s—the burlap that fronted the bar was eliminated and replaced with mahogany, which also replaced the knotty pine walls. By 1995, Wood owned the building, celebrating by having a "Lost Our Lease" party in which he burned the lease in the bar's eternal flame, which is kept in the office in a go-cup.

Wood still owns the bar today, and, as when it was founded back in the 1930s, it remains a home-away-from-home for gays and visitors to the Quarter. Caplinger, Barthel, and Collins would no doubt be thrilled that their legacy lives on.

Liz Kelley of Cure makes an Obituary Cocktail. Photo by Chris Granger.

CHAPTER TWO

HEAVEN KNOWS

INGREDIENTS

> There can be nothing more frequent than an occasional drink.
>
> —OSCAR WILDE

There are three basic ingredients to the Obituary Cocktail—gin, vermouth, and absinthe—all of which have, one could say, reputations. The fortunes of gin have changed through the ages, while vermouth can sometimes seem like an afterthought—and it shouldn't be. The rise and fall and rise of absinthe is worthy of an epic movie. Knowing the origins of these liquors provides context not only for the

Obituary Cocktail but for other drinks—and can make for great cocktail party conversation!

(Be sure to check out the Resources section at the end of this book for books and articles that go into depth about these liquors. I've written a condensed history here, and if you want to learn more, these publications will greatly enhance your liquor knowledge.)

GIN

At its most basic, gin is a distilled alcoholic drink flavored with juniper, various botanicals, and spices, which could include coriander, cardamom, angelica root, chamomile, elderflower, and orris root, among others.

The name "gin" is derived from the French word for juniper, *genièvre,* followed by the Dutch *genever* (or *jenever*), with roots in the Latin word for juniper, *juniperus.* It was the British who shortened it to gin circa 1714, but more on that later.

Juniper is gin's key ingredient—and gin is not gin unless juniper is in it. An aromatic evergreen shrub or tree of the cypress family, the *Juniperus* genus includes sixty to seventy species found in the Northern Hemisphere of Asia, Europe, and North America. Juniper's female seed cones look like berries, so in print or in any general reference about gin, "juniper berry" is sometimes used interchangeably with juniper. It is these "berries" that are used for gin.

IN THE BEGINNING

Juniper's value treating maladies was touted in the ancient world—and it probably was used this way even earlier. "Juniper has appeared whenever medicine has in history: In the Ebers Papyrus of Egypt, it is used along with coriander, poppy, wormwood and honey in a remedy 'by which the goddess Isis prepared for the god Ra to drive out the pains that are in his head,'" writes Camper English in *Doctors and Distillers: The Remarkable Medicinal History of Beer, Wine, Spirits and Cocktails*. Pliny was also quoted as recommending juniper berries "to cleanse the liver and kidneys." As time went on, juniper was also added to beer and other spirits to cure cough and cramps, among other conditions, and used as a diuretic.

Genever made its appearance in print in the 1260s, when Flemish poet Jacob van Maerlant (or Jacob van Maerlant te Damme) published *Der Naturen Bloeme,* a natural history encyclopedia that described how to add parts of the juniper tree to a spirit made of distilled wine, with the mixture intended for medicinal purposes. During the Black Death (ca. 1373–1600s), juniper berries were inserted into plague doctors' birdlike beaked masks because it was believed that good smells canceled out "miasma," the bad smells associated with decaying bodies and other odors thought to cause disease—and allegedly kept the doctor from being infected.

But for all this talk about genever's medicinal value, one also has to assume it wasn't only used this way once its other, more pleasurable effect was discovered. Geraldine Coates, editor of *Gintime,* says that even though there is no precise date or written record of when the transition from medicinal to drink occurred, it could most likely be found in taxes levied on distilleries from that time. She also pointed out that a number of tavern paintings from the fifteenth century suggest a love of spirits.

The first known recipe for genever made for nonmedicinal purposes dates back to 1495 in the Netherlands. According to *Doctors and Distillers,* the recipe was a "combination wine-and-beer base that was redistilled with juniper, nutmeg, cinnamon, galangal, grains of paradise, cloves, ginger, sage and cardamom."

The use of juniper continued to show up in publications such as in 1500, when physician Hieronymous Braunschweig wrote *Liber de arte destillandi,* in which a juniper *aqua vitae* appears. According to Coates in *Gintime,* it was in 1552, when *Een Constelijck Distilleer Boek* by Antwerp-based Philippus Hermanni was published, that the first recorded mention of genever as a distilled beverage flavored with juniper was mentioned.

In 1582, the use of grain as a base for distilling begins to appear in Casper Jansz Coolhaes's *A Guide to Distilling,* which uses the term "brandywine," aka *brandewijn,* when referencing French grapes that are distilled into burnt wine.

GIN ENTERS THE PICTURE

During the seventeenth century, among the different dynastic skirmishes that made up the Thirty Years' War (1618–48), troops from England were dispatched to Europe to support other Protestant nations, including the Dutch in their revolt against Spanish rule. When the British were there, they observed their Dutch compatriots drinking genever before going into battle, hence the phrase "Dutch courage" (aka "liquid courage"), as the liquor was said to bolster confidence. These British troops returned home with a taste for genever (it was also called geneva) and a yearning to re-create it at home.

Also dovetailing with this was the ascension of the Dutch Republic's William of Orange in 1689 as the ruler of England, Ireland, and Scotland, as King William III. He started ruling the Dutch Republic in 1672 and ruled both realms until his death in 1702.

While Dutch (or Holland) genever was imported, the government, in an attempt to bolster the British economy, introduced heavy taxes on imported beverages like French wine and brandy, and lowered taxes on grain distilleries

Gin Lane, from the pair of prints *Beer Street* and *Gin Lane,* by William Hogarth, etching and line engraving ca. 1750–51. Public Domain.

in England/Scotland/Ireland. At some point, the British started to shorten name, with the word "gin" first showing up in "The Fable of Bees: or, Private Vices, Publick Benefits," by Bernard Mandeville in 1714.

THE GIN CRAZE

Gin started replacing beer as the most popular consumed alcohol. Making its way through all facets of society, the "Gin Craze" started to take hold, reaching its peak between 1720 and the 1740s. Although Dutch genever was still being imported and local distilleries were making gin, the industry was unregulated, and pubs and people at home—with many using harmful ingredients, such as turpentine—made gin.

Gin shops also welcomed women to imbibe—something new to English society—and led to the London slums and elsewhere being overtaken by alcoholism in both sexes. It was estimated in 1730 that about seven thousand gin shops were in business in London, serving an estimated ten million gallons of gin, though some sources say three million. The attendant societal ills—including crime, violence, child abandonment (along with children also drinking gin), prostitution, mental illness, and, ultimately, death because of gin addiction—were not uncommon.

Enter artist and social commenter William Hogarth (1697–1764), who was known for his satirical engravings and paintings about eighteenth-century English society. His well-known engravings *Gin Lane* (1751) and *A Rake's Progress* (a series of eight paintings, 1732–34) depicted the ill effects of gin upon all levels of society. Upper-class society, itself addicted to gin, thought this only happened to the lower classes.

The British navy also got involved with the popularization of gin and helped inspire the term "Navy Strength," although much later (see following for gin types). Gin also acquired a few more nicknames during this time: "opium of the people," "Madam Geneva," "Ladies' Delight," "Cuckold's Comfort," and "Mother's Ruin," which allegedly was based on women neglecting their children and becoming prostitutes.

Although the British government tried to get a handle on the Gin Craze through a variety of taxes and laws throughout this time, it wasn't until 1751, when the Gin Act was passed, that a turnaround started. The act prohibited gin distillers from selling to unlicensed merchants and increased fees to merchants, thus eliminating the smaller gin shops and keeping the control of gin in the hands of larger distillers and retailers in Great Britain. The economy also changed around this time. Bad grain harvests forced prices up, and there was a decline in wages, so the poor weren't able to afford gin. By 1757, the Gin Craze was over.

Of note, gin's bad reputation came back during U.S. Prohibition (1920–33), when the scarcity of liquor—because it was outlawed—led to it being illegally concocted by amateurs in small quantities at home, giving rise to the nickname "bathtub gin." It was often bad as well, tainted with adulterated ingredients that could make a person ill or kill them. Cocktails became more popular as a way to mask the flavor of inferior alcohol. Among the cocktails credited to being invented during this time was the Bee's Knees, a mixture of gin, lemon juice, and honey.

Gin was also a favorite of the literary set, with F. Scott Fitzgerald and Ernest Hemingway extolling its charms during their time in Paris in the 1920s. Later, in the U.S., Fitzgerald preferred a Gin Rickey, and Hemingway liked dry martinis. In the 1950s and 1960s, Madison Avenue advertising types popularized the three-martini lunch. In the 1970s, gin began to lose popularity as that other clear spirit, vodka, started to gain it. But with cocktails enjoying a resurgence in popularity during the past twenty years, gin has been marching forward, with a number of new gin distillers experimenting and creating new fans.

Below is a list of the main types of gins with a brief history, some suggested brands, and a basic flavor profile (as there can be variations among these types).

GENEVER (OR JENEVER)

Genever is generally known for its neutral taste with a slight aroma of juniper and malt wine (though some say whiskey). Dutch in origin, it has a European Union and U.K. Protected Designation of Origin, which means the term "genever" can only be used if the product is made according to the specifications in Belgium, the Netherlands, two northern French areas, and two German federal states.

Brands: Bols (which has been producing the liquor since 1664), Boomsma, Anchor Genevieve

LONDON DRY

London Dry is a distilled gin made with juniper berries and botanicals or spices, which are added prior to the distillation process. European Union laws require that no synthetic botanicals be used. No sugar or sweeteners are allowed to be added.

After the botanicals are macerated, the gin is redistilled to produce a high-strength spirit. It is then diluted with water to reach the final proof. The London part of the name comes from the eighteenth century, when most dry gins were made in London, though that doesn't mean it has to be made in the city.

Brands: Booth's, Fords, Miles, Beefeater, Bombay Sapphire

PLYMOUTH

Considered to be on the earthier side, Plymouth features more citrus notes than a London Dry, of which Plymouth is considered an offshoot. The gin has been made by hand at the Blackfriars Distillery in Devon, England, since 1793. It uses the same recipe dating back two hundred years and is distilled in a single Victorian copper pot. It was the favorite gin of director Alfred Hitchcock and U.S. President Franklin D. Roosevelt.

Brand: Plymouth

OLD TOM

Slightly sweeter than London Dry, but less dry than Dutch genever, Old Tom gin started appearing in the 1800s, or maybe a little earlier. While there seem to be no clear clues to the origin of its name, in *Famous New Orleans Drinks and How to Mix 'Em,* author Stanley Clisby Arthur offers two theories: The first was that the gin got its name after an old tomcat fell into the barrel of spirits. The second, which may have been around longer than the gin-soaked cat, was that Hodges' Distillery in England (ca. 1780s–90s) named a brand of gin for one of their distillers, old Tom Chamberlain. Interestingly, Portobello Road Distillery found the recipe for the Hodges' Old Tom and re-created it as closely as possible. The label has "Old Tom" and a tomcat on it, so there may be a little bit of truth to both stories. Old Tom started disappearing from favor in the early part of the twentieth century but is making a comeback.

Brands: Portobello Road, Hayman Distillers, Tanqueray, Ransom Spirits

NAVY STRENGTH

Gin lovers can thank the British Royal Navy for laying the groundwork for this term in the eighteenth century. It only came into being in 1993, when Plymouth Gin coined the phrase. Generally, gin has an ABV (alcohol by volume) of 35–55 percent, whereas Navy Strength gin has at least 57.15 percent. So, technically, any gin of 57.15 percent ABV and above is a Navy Strength gin. Why so high? Gin and rum were stored in wooden barrels along with gunpowder below deck. Rum was the preferred ration for sailors; gin was reserved for the officers. As nothing was truly firmly sealed, gin and rum would leak and get the gunpowder wet. As such, gin had to be at least 57.15 percent ABV or else the gunpowder would not burn.

One of gin's most famous cocktails has its origins in India, when sailors took quinine, an antimalarial compound that tasted bitter, dissolved it in carbonated water to make tonic water, then added gin, thereby creating a gin and tonic. Today's tonic water only has trace amounts of quinine.

Brands: Fords Gin Officers' Reserve, Four Pillars Navy Strength Gin

SLOE GIN

The flavor of sloe gin is slightly sweet and botanical with a tartness from the sloe berries (a type of plum), with a lower alcohol content than traditional gin. Distillers started incorporating sloes in the seventeenth century. It starts as a traditionally made gin, but in this case, sloe berries, which are the fruit of the blackthorn tree, are harvested in the fall and added after the distillation process. This creates its distinct hue that can range from slightly pinkish to purple/red. Its famous cocktail is, of course, the Sloe Gin Fizz.

Brands: Fords, Plymouth, Hayman's, Sipsmith

VERMOUT DOLIN

CHAMBÉRY

LA PLUS ANCIENNE
FABRIQUE DE
VERMOUT DE
FRANCE
FONDÉE EN 1821

MEMBRE DU JURY
EXPOSITIONS UNIVERSELLES
PARIS 1900
MARSEILLE 1922

INVENTEUR DU VERMOUT DE CHAMBÉRY

IMP. GOUGENHEIM FR. LYON

VERMOUTH

When you ask the average person what vermouth is or what it is used for, the answer is most likely going to be, "It's something that goes into a martini." This is true, but it is so much more interesting than just an ingredient in a martini—or even an Obituary Cocktail.

At its most fundamental, vermouth is aromatized wine and is a subcategory of fortified wine. Vermouth hues can be anything from white to pale yellow to a deep red with flavors ranging from dry and herbaceous to strong, sweet, or sour. What is a fortified wine? It is a wine that has a distilled spirit usually added to increase alcohol content, thereby "fortifying" it. Other examples of fortified wines are port, sherry, and madeira. An aromatized wine is a fortified wine that has also been flavored with botanicals, spices, and other natural additives. Vermouths also generally have an ABV of 15–22 percent, which is higher than most unfortified wines of 9–14 percent ABV.

Opposite: Advertisement for Dolin vermouth from the 1930s. Courtesy of the Dolin Company.

One notable additive, wormwood, gave vermouth its name: the German word for the herb is *Wermut.* "Vermouth" reflects the French pronunciation of the German word. If wormwood sounds familiar, it is probably because of its Latin name: *Artemisia absinthium,* grand wormwood, and its use in absinthe. The *Artemisia* genus contains many species, and *Artemisia pontica* (Roman wormwood; small wormwood) is perhaps most associated with vermouth.

Wormwood has been added to wine since Ancient Greece (though honestly, it may go back further), when Hippocrates macerated wine with wormwood and other spices or botanicals to create medicinal elixirs. Wormwood was believed to be effective in treating stomach disorders and intestinal parasites.

Romans were known for their wormwood wines and probably helped spread its popularity as its troops criss-crossed Europe while they were conquering the region. In the sixteenth century, a merchant named D'Alessio who lived in the Piedmont region of today's Italy began producing a wormwood wine in which he introduced more botanicals. France started producing its own wormwood wines with unique combinations of botanicals, and by the mid-seventeenth century, the drink was being consumed in England as vermouth.

Over time, the two versions of vermouth were established: sweet (red) and dry. It was wine shop owner Antonio Benedetto Carpano who, in 1786, introduced the first sweet (red) vermouth. Carpano studied to be an herbalist, which led him to experiment with combining herbs and spices with muscatel wine. His shop, located in Turin, Italy (then part of the Kingdom of Sardinia), was opposite the Royal Palace. One day, he sent over a crate of bottles filled with a new concoction of vermouth to King Vittorio Amedeo III. The king liked it so much that it became a regular libation at court.

Dry vermouth came not too long after: sometime between 1800 to 1813, the first pale, dry vermouth was produced in France

Bottle of Dolin's dry vermouth. Courtesy of the Dolin Company.

by Joseph Noilly. But wait, there is one more type of vermouth to take note of: blanco, or blanc, vermouth, which was said to have been invented in the late nineteenth century in Chambéry in southeastern France.

As the years went on, vermouth evolved from something medicinal to drink to being served as an aperitif, particularly in Italy and France. By the late nineteenth century, it was appearing in cocktails, such as the Manhattan, which was invented sometime in the 1870s or 1880s. But unlike its alcohol brethren such as vodka, gin, or rum, vermouth did not acquire the same sort of popularity in the U.S. as it had in Europe.

The tides have been changing over time due to the quality of vermouths and the rising popularity of its use as a cocktail ingredient. "Using a good-quality vermouth is critical," said Bryan Dias, cocktail expert and host of *NOLADrinks Show,* a podcast and website (noladrinks.com). Dias is also a vermouth evangelist. "For the longest time, there were a number of cheap vermouths available and not very interesting ones available in the U.S.," said Dias. Now, he adds, the options are much better.

And with those options come myriad choices that could be confusing. "It's important to become familiar with the styles of vermouth, as the flavor profile varies because of the different botanicals used in each," he said. "Trust your palate."

Once the delights of vermouth—good vermouth—are sampled, sipping into the sunset with it either mixed with a good club soda or with gin and absinthe à la the Obituary Cocktail could become an evening ritual.

No matter the type, vermouth must start with the same base of a neutral white grape, consist of at least 75 percent wine, and contain *Artemisia.*

DRY VERMOUTH

Dry vermouth has a mild herbal flavor and can have floral and fruit notes. It is usually from France. It can be less bitter than sweet vermouth. This type of vermouth often contains no added sugar and is limited by the European Union to have a maximum sugar content of 50 grams per liter. Extra dry vermouth has even less: 30 grams maximum per liter.

This type of vermouth is mostly used in a martini and Obituary Cocktail.

Brands: Dolin, Noilly Prat

SWEET (RED) VERMOUTH

Usually from Italy, sweet (red) vermouth—also called Rosso—gets its color from a variety of sources: red wine, botanicals, and often caramel (what Martini & Rossi uses). Sweet vermouth has a bolder flavor than dry vermouth. It has a minimum sugar content of 130 grams per liter as per the European Union.

It is used mainly in a Manhattan and Negroni.

Brands: Martini & Rossi, Dolin, Cocchi di Torino, Carpano Antica

BLANCO VERMOUTH

This type of white vermouth falls between dry and sweet vermouth and is sometimes called semidry. It can offer vanilla or honey-like notes in its flavor. It has a sugar content of 50–90 grams per liter.

It is often made as an aperitif or topped off with soda. Brands: Dolin, Contratto

HOW TO STORE VERMOUTH— IT'S IMPORTANT

Many a vermouth has been ruined by being stored incorrectly—just like my parents did, who used to keep it in their liquor cabinet, which was totally the wrong thing to do. One important thing to remember is that vermouth is a wine. And like wine or liquor, if it isn't stored properly, it degrades more quickly. Then, when it is used in a cocktail, well, of course, it isn't going to taste like it should. Another factor to consider is that because vermouth is low ABV (generally 15–22 percent), it won't last as long as a higher ABV alcohol.

Bryan Dias said that vermouth, after it has been opened, needs to be kept in either a wine refrigerator or a regular refrigerator. "There are varying schools of thought on how long it will last," said Dias, "but in my mind, I try to consume mine within three to four weeks all while being

DOLIN DOLIN
DRY
DOLIN
Maison fondée en 1821
VERMOUTH
DE
CHAMBÉRY
RHÔNE-ALPES
DU VERMOUTH DE CHAMBÉRY – MAISON
Louis Ferdinand Dolin
PRODUIT ET MIS EN BOUTEILLE A CHAMBÉRY (FRANCE)

stored in the refrigerator." He added, "Refrigeration can greatly increase the time it will last, perhaps doubling it," citing a test by Tasting Table. Dias said using a wine-saver pump can also help to a certain extent, as it removes most of the air from an open bottle of vermouth, slowing down the oxidization and degradation.

If you occasionally use vermouth, an option Dias noted was that a number of brands are now making 375 ml. (half) bottles of vermouth, so there isn't as much waste. Then again, there is always the fallback to vermouth a bit past its prime: use it in cooking as it adds a wonderful flavor to dishes.

ABSINTHE

Ah, absinthe, the bad boy (or girl) of the spirit world. Never has a liquor—except for that one you had a bad experience with in college—had such a reputation.

Opposite: Martini made with Dolin vermouth. Courtesy of the Dolin Company.

ALCOHOLIC BEVER GE TAX
FRAPPE SLOWLY IN LARGE GLASS WITH CRUSHED ICE & SELTZER OR CARBONATED WATER UNTIL LIQUID OPALIZES
FOR ABSINTHE
ANISETTE
ADD SMALL QUANTITY
ANISETTE OR SIMPLE
SYRUP AND PROCEED
AS OPPOSITE
ABSINTHE
DISTILLED BY
L.E. JUNG & WULFF CO., INC.
NEW ORLEANS, LA.
SERVE IN SMALL GLASS STRAINED FREE OF ICE
ALCOHOL ABOUT 120 PROOF 60% BY VOL
SINCE 1883

But before we get to how absinthe got such a reputation—and why these misconceptions started—let's start with what it actually is.

Absinthe is a high-proof spirit distilled with sweet fennel, green anise (its dominant flavor), and the flowers of the grand wormwood, *Artemisia absinthium*. Depending on the brand, it can also include other herbs.

It is typically 90–148 proof and 45–74 percent ABV, which makes it an overproof liquor, a spirit with an ABV more than 50 percent. It can be, depending on how it is made, colorless to varying shades of green.

Absinthe's most famous ingredient, wormwood, has been used medicinally since ancient Egypt, around 1550 BC, when it was mentioned in the Ebers Papyrus. Wormwood continued to be used medicinally through the ages, treating ailments, mainly with issues affecting digestion such as worms, or as an antiseptic and treating fevers, making it a sort of cure-all.

Opposite: Jung & Wulff Co. Absinthe label. Jung and Wulff distilled at 317–19 Magazine Street between 1883 and 1912. Photo courtesy Phillip Collier.

Wormwood also contains a chemical called thujone, which, when consumed in large quantities, can act as a convulsant. In small quantities, like in a few servings of absinthe, thujone is not an issue. Remember this chemical, as it will become important later in absinthe's history.

When absinthe, as the liquor, first appeared is open to conjecture. But, as early as 1639, a medicinal drink published in the *The Distiller of London,* a tome for doctors, contained a recipe called *Aqua Absinthii* for common wormwood and anise (which can also be called aniseed), distilled and sweetened with sugar, which, if you are a fan of absinthe, sounds familiar.

While who invented it is still a mystery, there are two commonly held theories that actually dovetail for the beginning of commercial production of the liquor. One says absinthe was made in Val-de-Travers, Switzerland, by the Henriod sisters and was then promoted by Pierre Ordinaire, a French doctor who had moved to Couvet, Switzerland (near Val-de-Travers), in 1767 in exile from France. Another theory has it the other way around: Dr. Ordinaire created absinthe, but the Henriod sisters promoted it.

Adding more confusion to the origin story, in 1769 a newspaper in the French-speaking Swiss Canton of Neuchâtel was advertising absinthe but listing it as an extract.

What is generally agreed upon by absinthe historians is that the recipe was sold in 1797 to Major Daniel-Henri Dubied, who was the first one to commercialize it. Dubied founded an absinthe distillery that same year in Couvet with his son, Marcellin Dubied, and son-in-law, Henri-Louis Perrenoud, and called it Dubied Père et Fils.

As absinthe gained in popularity, the son-in-law—hoping to capitalize on the burgeoning French market and to avoid paying French taxes at the border—moved in 1805 to Pontarlier, France, shortened his last name to Pernod, and started distilling absinthe at his Pernod Fils distillery. The Pernod brand still exists today.

But wait, yes, there is another story about how absinthe started being commercially produced. In *The Absinthe Frappé,* Marielle Songy revealed that Abram-Louis Perrenoud, the father of Henri-Louis Perrenoud, is thought to have been the first to distill absinthe in Couvet, circa 1774.

In an interview Songy did with absinthe expert Ted Breaux, he added, "The nature of his association with Major Dubied at this time seems to be unclear. Dubied may have been a partner and financier, with Perrenoud in charge of operations. Perrenoud's untimely death precipitated a chain of events that muddy the waters." After that it is unclear if Henri-Louis Perrenoud took over his father's shares in the company, or if Dubied received them.

THE RISE OF LA FÉE VERTE (THE GREEN FAIRY)

Absinthe was gaining admirers, and by the time the mid-nineteenth century came around, absinthe was creeping its way into different facets of French society. In the 1830s and 1840s, soldiers who were stationed in Algeria, which France had invaded, were supplied with rations of absinthe to help purify water against bacteria that caused dysentery, among other diseases, and they may have used it as a malaria preventative. Once back home, the soldiers continued to drink absinthe.

It was around this time that the "Green Hour," akin to today's happy hour, took hold, with the elite of French society taking sips of absinthe—and no doubt some other liquors—between 5:00 and 7:00 p.m. as a precursor to dinner. If it was considered bad form to drink "The Green Fairy"—a name based on absinthe's green hue—after dinner, few cared.

Bohemian society also took a liking to this liquor, with artists Vincent Van Gogh, Edgar Degas, and Henri Toulouse-Lautrec imbibing, while some also depicted it in art, as in Édouard Manet's *The Absinthe Drinker,* Degas's *L'Absinthe,* and Van Gogh's *Café Table with Absinthe.* Authors Oscar Wilde, Paul-Marie Verlaine, and Paul Rimbaud were known to favor the liquor.

In addition to its increasing popularity among French citizens in the following decades, two other factors helped absinthe become more available to the masses. The distillation process for alcohol was moving away from an alembic still, which could only make batches, to a column still, which allowed for the continuous distillation, and thereby faster production, of high-proof spirits. The base of absinthe started to change as well. The traditional spirit base of eau-de-vie distilled from grapes was being replaced by sugar beets, molasses, or grain. These were thought to be of lower quality, and when combined with ingredients that weren't of a high grade, such as adding wormwood oil instead of actually distilling wormwood, an inferior product was made. This process was cheaper, and profiteers started producing adulterated imitations.

By the 1850s, Pernod Fils was producing about twenty thousand liters per day, and at its height, thirty thousand liters per day. More factors also came into play in making absinthe more popular: it has a higher ABV of 45–74 percent, so getting drunk was easier and less expensive. And some, depending upon exactly what and how much of it they drank, alleged it caused hallucinations.

Sales of absinthe were beginning to outpace France's other drink of choice, wine. And that's when the trouble started. Actually, what kicked it off was French vineyards becoming infected in the 1860s and 1870s with phylloxera, an insect that attacks grape plants' roots, which destroyed most of the country's wine industry. With wine prices increasing, and absinthe now using ingredients other than wine for its base spirit and its prices decreasing, this green-tinted spirit began catching on.

Wine producers were not happy and started a campaign against the liquor, promoting the theory that wine was good for you and actually cured alcoholism, or what was also called "absinthism." As the wine industry started to recover, it also began saying that wine was natural and made with good-quality ingredients, whereas absinthe was "artificial." Wine manufacturers also worked with the French temperance movement to discourage absinthe drinking, arguing that wine didn't cause alcoholism.

At the turn of the nineteenth century, anti-absinthe forces started to gain traction, with absinthe's namesake ingredient, *Artemisia absinthium,* and its constituents (e.g., thujone) as the target. While thujone is present in properly distilled absinthe only in traces, an excessive amount can cause convulsions, renal failure, and death. Modern-day studies of vintage absinthe demonstrated that it typically contained 0–48 ppm of thujone. Today, in the U.S., the maximum limit for thujone is 10 ppm; in the U.K. and Europe, the maximum is 35 ppm.

But back in 1905, what bolstered anti-absinthe forces was when Swiss laborer Jean Lanfray murdered his pregnant wife and their daughters in an alleged absinthe fury, which was most likely the result of alcoholism, a bad temper, and a daylong bender. It was reported that Lanfray's day had started with absinthe, then progressed to coffee, brandy, crème de menthe, and cognac mixed with soda, as well as seven glasses of wine, and ended with coffee and brandy. An argument with his wife about polishing his boots that had started earlier in the day was revived, and in response, he loaded his rifle and shot her, then their young daughters. He tried to commit suicide but failed, only shooting himself in the jaw.

He didn't remember what had happened, but the newspapers somehow ascertained what he had drunk, focusing on the absinthe and blaming it for the murders. He was convicted of the murders, sentenced to thirty years' imprisonment, then committed suicide three days later in jail.

A petition was signed by 34,375 men and 48,075 women for the immediate ban of absinthe. Belgium jumped on that ban bandwagon in 1905, and Switzerland followed suit in 1910. From there it got progressively worse for absinthe: Holland banned it in 1910, the U.S. in 1912, France in 1915, and Germany in 1923. It was, however, never formally banned in the U.K., Spain, Sweden, Portugal, Czech Republic, or Norway. Absinthe continued to be produced in Spain, Portugal, and later in the Czech Republic.

Note that even with this ban, the desire for anise-flavored liquor remained with pastis from France, arak from Lebanon, Chinchón from Spain, ouzo from Greece, raki from Turkey, sambuca from Italy, and Xtabentún from Mexico, among the choices. Also note that these are not good substitutes for absinthe in cocktails.

Prohibition in the U.S. provided another blow to absinthe when it kicked off in the U.S. in 1920. The Volstead Act, as it was called, prohibited the manufacture, transport, and sale of alcohol. Even with the absinthe ban and Prohibition, two men in New Orleans were coming up with an absinthe substitute.

NEW ORLEANS AND ABSINTHE—PLUS HERBSAINT

Absinthe made its first recorded appearance in New Orleans in an 1837 ad. Was it already in the city? Probably. Given the city's French and Spanish roots, it's not surprising that this liquor became popular. As time went on, the city became known as the "Little Paris of America," as well as the absinthe capital of North America.

Some of that absinthe went into making the Sazerac, a cocktail long associated with the city. In *The Sazerac,* author Tim McNally shares the recipe for the Sazerac: cognac, absinthe, simple syrup, and Peychaud's bitters. He notes that absinthe wasn't used in the initial Sazerac but started appearing in the 1850s.

Cayetano Ferrér played an important part in the New Orleans absinthe story. In 1869, he was hired away from the French Opera House by the Aleix Brothers for their

Legendre Herbsaint advertisements. Courtesy of Sazerac Company Archives.

new coffeehouse—at that time, coffeehouses also served liquor—on the corner of Bourbon and Bienville Streets. Ferrér was a hit, particularly with his creation the Absinthe Frappé, a mixture of absinthe, simple syrup, and soda water with mint for a garnish. In 1874, he leased the building, originally built in 1806, and named it the Absinthe Room. Today the bar is known as the Old Absinthe House, where you can still see the nineteenth-century marble fountains used to drip cool water into glasses of absinthe.

There were a number of New Orleans distilleries that made absinthe, or variations thereof, in New Orleans, including A. M. & J. Solari Greenopal and J. C. Yochim Co. Inc., which made an absinthe and interestingly had another offering of Liquere D'Elite, which is actually arak, an anise-flavored liquor.

More is known about L. E. Jung, who started his distillery in 1883. Once the ban on absinthe hit the U.S. in 1912, Jung changed his formula, which now lacked wormwood, and called it Greenopal, which seems to be the name used for absinthe "substitute" liquor. Jung died in 1926, and Fred Wulff bought the distillery, renaming it L. E. Jung & Wulff

Legendre Herbsaint advertisement on building at the corner of Canal and N. Rampart Streets, 1934. Courtesy of Sazerac Company Archives.

Company. Once Prohibition was repealed, the distillery started producing Jung & Wulff Absinthe, which had no wormwood in it. Once the Federal Alcohol Control Commission caught wind of this, it made the distillery delete "absinthe" from its name. The resulting product's new name was Milky Way.

There is, of course, a more famous absinthe-minus-wormwood liquor than the one produced by Jung & Wulff:

Herbsaint. New Orleanian Joseph Marion Legendre and Australian Reginald Parker met in France in the midst of World War I (1914–18), where at some point they learned how to make absinthe. Parker moved to New Orleans, popped into the Legendre family pharmacy, and the two then started experimenting, as ingredients were readily available and the pharmacy had a federal license to sell alcohol by prescription.

But it took some time for the new alcohol business, J. M. Legendre & Company, to officially sell the liquor—it wasn't until post-Prohibition in 1934 that Herbsaint (from French Creole *herb santé,* meaning sacred herb) hit the market. According to Songy's *The Absinthe Frappé,* it was originally labeled "Legendre Absinthe," even though an absinthe substitute, Herbsaint, was used. Once again, the Federal Alcohol Control Commission objected to "Absinthe" in the name, because not only was the liquor still not legal, but it also wasn't absinthe. Thus, "Legendre Herbsaint" was born.

One main difference between absinthe and Herbsaint is that the latter contains no grand wormwood. It does,

Ads for Herbsaint. Courtesy of Sazerac Company Archives

however, have the anise flavor associated with absinthe, which makes Herbsaint a frequent substitute for absinthe in cocktails.

Both Jung & Wulff (which had been bought by George Benz & Sons in 1940) and J. M. Legendre & Company are now owned by the New Orleans–based Sazerac Company.

ABSINTHE GOES LEGAL IN THE U.S.

The movement to legalize absinthe, or at least reintroduce it, began gaining momentum in the early 1990s. George Rowley is credited with bringing it back in the U.K., where it was never formally banned but was hard to find. He started the process in the mid-1990s, getting import approval in 1998. Unfortunately, the U.K. market became saturated with inferior absinthe, so he went about creating his own: La Fée Parisienne, the first grand wormwood absinthe to be distilled in France since the 1915 ban, was first bottled in 2000.

Back in the U.S., one of liquor's proponents, New Orleanian Ted Breaux, was bitten by the absinthe bug during the early 1990s. Determined to prove the science behind the ban was wrong, he reverse engineered preban absinthes. This included a bottle of vintage Pernod Tarragona (the company's distillery in Spain), which he purchased in 1996 for three hundred dollars from Lucullus Antiques in New Orleans, and a bottle that was almost one hundred years old by Édouard Pernod, a find via a friend. Breaux also came upon fake absinthe from the Czech Republic, where it was often artificially dyed green, though some versions could be red, yellow, blue, or black.

In 2000, Breaux became the first person to analyze samples of the vintage absinthe, which revealed it was high in alcohol volume and contained nothing else considered to be harmful. He founded Jade Liqueurs, and, in early 2004, he started distilling absinthe that was close to what a nineteenth-century gentleman or gentlewoman would have sipped. His Jade absinthes continue to be distilled at the historic Combier Distillery in France.

Absinthe wasn't legal again in the U.S. until Breaux and his partners at Viridian Spirits convinced the U.S. government's Alcohol and Tobacco Tax and Trade Bureau to lift the ban on March 5, 2007, which saw the launch of Lucid absinthe. Kübler, a Swiss brand instrumental in lifting the ban in Switzerland in 2005 and engaged in U.S. government discussions, obtained approval in May of that same year. March 5 is now recognized as "National Absinthe Day." Today, there are a number of absinthes on the market, including the ones made by Atelier Vie in New Orleans.

HOW TO ENJOY ABSINTHE IN THE OBITUARY COCKTAIL

Absinthe is a strong ingredient—I tried batching the cocktail based proportionally to the traditional Obituary Cocktail recipe. It doesn't work, as the absinthe dominates the drink flavors as it sits. When not the main ingredient in a drink, such as the Absinthe Frappé, it is best used as an accent for a cocktail, a point emphasized in *The Mixologist,* by Cincinnati hotelier C. F. Lawler. In this book published in 1895, he writes that a small amount of absinthe frequently improves the flavor of a cocktail. Ted Breaux concurs, saying he applies absinthe much like a "cocktail hot sauce."

The absinthe in an Obituary Cocktail can be just a "wash," or spray, on the glass or on top of the drink—much like the "cocktail hot sauce"—or it can be a more substantial ingredient. As with any drink, it may take some time to figure out your preference.

There is an absinthe display within the Southern Food and Beverage Museum/Museum of the American Cocktail in New Orleans. La Galerie d'Absinthe is full of ephemera about the liquor collected by absinthe expert Ray Bordelon and other donors.

St. Roch's Chapel and cemetery in New Orleans, LA, ca. 1900–1906. Detroit Publishing Company Photograph Collection, Library of Congress Prints and Photographs Division.

CHAPTER THREE

SIX FEET UNDER

DEATH TRADITIONS IN NEW ORLEANS

> Rejoice at the death and cry at the birth:
> New Orleans sticks close to the Scriptures.
>
> —JELLY ROLL MORTON

Ever since Jean-Baptiste Le Moyne de Bienville set foot in 1699 on Louisiana soil (no, he wasn't in New Orleans proper; he was much farther south), explorers and colonizers have grappled with many of the region's daunting elements—blazingly hot weather, mosquitoes (and the accompanying diseases), alligators, snakes, quicksand, floods, and a lack of fresh water—with death looming large as an end result. It wasn't a hospitable environment for those new to the shores—or even to the Native American inhabitants already there.

It took time for the city to beat epidemics and recover (as much as it could) from wars and other natural and man-made disasters to reach some sense of stability. Even with that, traditions surrounding death—its sadness and celebration—persevered. And, like many New Orleans cultural touchstones, these traditions are a mélange of the cultures of Native American, the enslaved, colonizers, and immigrants.

BULBANCHA, NEW ORLEANS, THE EARLY YEARS

Native Americans, who had been at the site along the Mississippi River now called the French Quarter for thousands of years, recognized the location's importance: it was relatively high among the surrounding, lower-lying swamps and was situated between the river and Lake Pontchartrain, both of which connected to the Gulf of Mexico. They would portage their boats between the Mississippi River site (where Conti Street is now) to Bayou St. John, which fed into the lake. The route to the Gulf of Mexico via the lake, which opens up to the gulf, was considered safer than the river.

Among the Native American tribes populating this area were the Chitimatcha, Ishak, Tunica, and Natchez, as well as the Choctaw, who named the future French Quarter "Bulbancha," (or "Balbancha"), meaning a "place of many tongues" or "the place of foreign tongues." By 1675, the Oumas Indians sold or traded goods with explorers, trappers, and Native Americans at the site now known as the French Market.

In 1682, René-Robert Cavelier, Sieur de La Salle, came down the Mississippi River from present-day Illinois. He may have stopped at Bulbancha, but he had other things on his mind, such as his claim of the Mississippi basin for France and naming it Louisiana after King Louis XIV. La Salle was also directionally challenged: when trying to find the river again from the Gulf of Mexico, he ended up in Texas—and was assassinated by his own men.

In 1698, Bienville and his brother, Pierre Le Moyne d'Iberville, both of whom had already been exploring the Gulf coast of Mississippi and Alabama, left French shores and landed in Mississippi, establishing Fort Maurepas (today's Ocean Springs, Mississippi). The brothers continued to explore the Mississippi River valley, and on March 2, 1699, Bienville landed on a plot of land sixty miles south of New Orleans, naming it "Pointe du Mardi Gras," as it was the eve of the holiday.

During his explorations, Bienville liked "the beautiful crescent along the river," as he wrote later in 1717, and persuaded the French government to propose a settlement there. Meanwhile, his brother, Iberville, was amenable to a site on Lake Pontchartrain and wanted to start a settlement on Bayou St. John. Bienville won out, and he named the settlement La Nouvelle-Orléans in honor of Phillip II, Duke d'Orleans, in France, also the then regent of France. The year was 1718.

The town was designed in a military-style city street plan by engineer and cartographer Adrien de Pauger, who was working with Pierre Le Blond de Tour. The street plan remains today: the boundaries are Rampart Street, Esplanade Avenue, Canal Street, and Decatur Street/the river. Pauger convinced Bienville to move the city front closer—seven hundred feet—to the river to what is now Decatur Street. Nature was not kind to the budding colony. A hurricane in 1722 leveled the buildings, but a levee subsequently built along the Mississippi River lessened the threat.

Many people, of course, died. It is believed that some of the earliest burials took place at the river's edge. One of the first known established burial grounds was the St. Peter Street Cemetery, which was created in 1722 or 1723. This in-ground cemetery was bounded by N. Rampart, St. Peter, Burgundy, and Toulouse Streets. Part of this site was where the old Mama Rosa's restaurant was; it is now a new condominium building. The cemetery was moved in 1801.

(Where cemeteries were located, property transfers, and more can be found in the New Orleans City Archives, which the Spanish government formally established on February 23, 1773. The Orleans Parish Clerk of Court office has records dating back to 1735.)

At this time, the city had not started constructing aboveground tombs. But, with the high-level water table and the sanitation issues cemeteries posed, the government ultimately turned to the Old World for a solution. St. Louis Cemetery No. 1, the first aboveground cemetery, was established by Spanish royal decree on August 14, 1789, and was located outside of the city's fortifications. It replaced the St. Peter Street Cemetery, which had become overcrowded.

Aboveground tombs originated in the Mediterranean region thousands of years ago, according to the Lafayette Cemetery Research Project. So, when the Spanish and French arrived in New Orleans, the tradition of aboveground burial tombs—*tumba* in Spanish, *tombeau* or *tombe* in French—they were aware of the tradition. In those countries the rocky soil probably made building a tomb a sensible choice.

In New Orleans, it was a status symbol to have a family tomb where multiple generations were laid to rest rather than being placed in-ground burial plots. There were also tombs for benevolent society members—and the members of various societies, social aid and pleasure clubs, religious groups, and fraternal organizations—with the multilevel tombs offering the entombment option to those who couldn't afford a family tomb. St. Louis No. 1 was initially only for Roman Catholics, although Protestant burials were allowed adjacent and in the back beginning in 1804.

These "Cities of the Dead," a phrase credited to Mark Twain from his *Life on the Mississippi* (1883), grew to include more aboveground cemeteries. St. Louis Cemetery No. 1, No. 2, and No. 3, Lafayette Cemetery No. 1 and No. 2, as well as the Metairie Cemetery are among the aboveground cemeteries people can see today.

Native Americans, such as the Choctaw, had their own version of aboveground tombs. In the 1700s, the Choctaws' ceremony for the dead involved a number traditions, including a period of mourning that could last four months or more. Bone pickers—designated men and sometimes women—would say when the mourning period was over. The bone pickers, distinguished by certain tattoos and nails that were long on their thumbs, forefingers, and middle fingers, would clean the flesh off of the bones, which were then placed into a box. A feast for the family and acquaintances would then take place, followed by taking the box to the family's charnel house, which was rectangular in shape and raised, where the bones were placed among those of their ancestors. As the Choctaw charnel houses filled with bones, the older bones were cleared out and buried in small, conical earth mounds. (For in-depth information about Choctaw burial practices, look at Iti Fabvssa, *Biskinik* online.)

In New Orleans, this last process was a little different in that after a year—or what the law prescribed—the aboveground tomb was opened and the coffin broken and burned. The remains were placed back into the crypt, usually in the back, or put into a caveau, located at ground level.

In November, Choctaws would go to the charnel house

for a Feast of the Dead, where they honored and celebrated their deceased ancestors. It's a tradition that dovetails with the Mexican Day of the Dead, usually November 1 and 2, and that goes back about three thousand years to pre-Columbian Mesoamerica. All Saints' Day, November 1, and All Souls' Day, November 2, are Christian celebrations honoring the dead that evolved out of paganism. In New Orleans on All Saints' Day, families go visit their ancestors, clean up, do maintenance work, as well as leave gifts.

FEVERS, EPIDEMICS, DEATH

It wasn't until 1854 that the connection between contaminated water and certain diseases was made, courtesy of Dr. John Snow in London, who uncovered the link. Cholera was among the diseases caused by contaminated water, and cholera epidemics occurred in New Orleans in 1832–33, 1848–55, 1866, and 1873. New Orleans lost more than seventeen thousand people to the disease during these periods.

The year 1900 was when the connection between yellow fever and mosquitoes was made. Once again, water played a part: mosquitoes breed in standing water. More than forty-one thousand people died from yellow fever in New Orleans between 1817 (when reliable sources emerged), with certain years as epidemic, and 1905, the last epidemic in the U.S. An outbreak in 1878 killed four thousand people in New Orleans.

Yellow fever's primary victims were immigrants, children, laborers, and the poor, as well as Native Americans. Even though the wealthy could escape the city during the months deemed dangerous, June to November (coincidentally hurricane season), escaping the disease could prove elusive. At some point in the nineteenth century, so many were dying that city residents were predicting that "pretty soon people will have to dig their own graves."

Opposite: Funeral of New Orleans musician John Frank Casimir, featuring Fats Houston, Grand Marshal of the Eureka Brass Band, and Bill Matthews as the first pallbearer, 1963. Alexander Allison Photograph Collection, City Archives and Special Collections, New Orleans Public Library.

BURIAL MARCHES, JAZZ FUNERALS, SECOND LINES

Second lines and jazz funerals are cultural phenomena found only in New Orleans. They were born of a number of traditions—African, Native American, European, Central American, Haitian, and the Caribbean—that were mainly coalesced by the city's Black population.

Jazz funerals have roots in West African Yoruba rituals; Black brass bands, social aid and pleasure clubs, and benevolent societies; the Catholic Church, Black churches (Catholic and Protestant); and Haitian Vodou's reverence for ancestral spirits. Also influencing them were the Native Americans funeral processionals and the city's Sicilian and southern Italian immigrants, who brought the tradition of a brass band with a funeral procession with them to the U.S.

One of the first burial marches in an established New Orleans was in 1789 for King Carlos III, when the city was controlled by Spain. In the nineteenth and early twentieth centuries, funding for funerals in New Orleans came from membership in a benevolent society (which were not limited to just the Black community but also included trades and a variety of ethnicities), and social aid clubs were established to help members afford a proper burial, medical bills, life insurance, and other necessities.

There are two parts of a jazz funeral: the mournful procession to the cemetery (the first line) and then the joyous return from it (the second line). Today, the second line's first line is the main section of the parade—the society's members, whomever is being honored, and the brass band—at a funeral it would include a hearse, with the second line made up of the people following the parade, usually dancing. "Jazz funeral" as a term didn't come into use until the 1930s, some say later.

The clubs would often have their own brass band. In 1875, the Société d'Economie et d'Assistance Mutuelle, a Black benevolent society, held a meeting and deemed the official music to be "brass band" music. During the late nineteenth century, the second line became its own tradition separate from the jazz funeral (although both can still occur together).

Today, social aid and pleasure clubs and benevolent societies have second lines on Sunday afternoons between September through May, avoiding the hot summer months.

CHAPTER FOUR

STIFF COMPETITION

EIGHT COCKTAILS WITH MORBID APPEAL

Drinking is a way of ending the day.

—ERNEST HEMINGWAY

The Obituary Cocktail is in good company with drinks bestowed with deathly monikers. Whether their names attest to a dark humor among their creators or to the power of the spirits, or are just clever tags dreamed up under spiritual power, drinks such as the Corpse Bride, Corpse

Reviver, Death in the Afternoon, Esprit de Corpse, Kill Devil, The Resurrection, Vampire's Kiss, and Zombie are an entryway to another realm. And who doesn't need some divine intervention or inspiration now and then?

BARREL-RESTED CORPSE REVIVER

SERVES 1

Courtesy Liz Kelley at Cure

¾ ounce Gravier Barrel-Rested Gin

¾ ounce Cointreau

¾ ounce Tempus Fugit Kina

¾ ounce Fresh lemon

Jade Nouvelle-Orléans Absinthe

Build all in a tin, except for the absinthe, with ice, then shake. Season a chilled cocktail glass with four sprays of absinthe. Double-strain the above mixture into the absinthe-seasoned coupe.

ABOUT CURE: Cure was opened in 2009 in New Orleans by Neal Bodenheimer, Matthew Kohnke, and Kirk Estopinal. It quickly became the place to be seen and the scene for cocktails, and it is largely credited for pioneering the modern-day craft cocktail movement in New Orleans. The bar/restaurant was recognized for its efforts by being named the 2018 winner of the James Beard Award for "Outstanding Bar Program," one of "America's Best Bars" by *Esquire,* and one of the "Best Cocktail Bars in the U.S." by *Food & Wine.*

CORPSE BRIDE

SERVES 1

Courtesy Gilded Perch, ParkView Historic Hotel

1½ ounces Empress 1908 Gin

¾ ounce St. Germain Elderflower Liqueur

¾ ounce lemon juice

3 drops 80/20 saline solution

Brut champagne

Absinthe Ordinaire

Lemon twist

Shake above ingredients, except absinthe, over ice and strain into a champagne flute spritzed two to three times (can be adjusted for taste) with absinthe. Top with a brut champagne and garnish with a lemon twist.

ABOUT THE GILDED PERCH BAR: The bar is nestled inside the ParkView Historic Hotel, a family-run boutique inn in New Orleans that dates to 1884. The Corpse Bride was born on a slow night in 2024 at the Gilded Perch, when bar manager William King, bartender Dr. Benji Creel, and Creel's fiancée (now wife) Denise were experimenting with a fun New Orleans cocktail for their upcoming nuptials. (The drink was a hit at the wedding.)

DEATH IN THE AFTERNOON

SERVES 1

Courtesy Liam Deegan, Barrel Proof

1 ounce or 1½ ounces Pernod Absinthe, chilled

4½ ounces Laurent-Perrier Brut Champagne, chilled

Lemon peel

Chill the absinthe in a mixing glass with ice and stir. Add to glass—either a small flute or coupe—then add chilled champagne. It will create an opalescent, milky look. Finish with a lemon peel.

* * *

Liam Deegan's fondness for this cocktail comes about because "I am not crazy about a straight martini," and he likes its link to Ernest Hemingway's *Death in the Afternoon,* a nonfiction book written in 1932 about bullfighting in Spain. Hemingway also used the title for his libationary contribution to *So Red the Nose, or Breath in the Afternoon*, by Sterling North and Carl Kroch, a cocktail book published in 1935 that featured recipes, some tongue-in-cheek, from leading authors of the day such as Edgar Rice Burroughs [creator of "Tarzan"] with their cocktails inspired by their books or something else.

According to *So Red the Nose . . . ,* the drink came about when the author and three officers of the HMS *Danae* "spent seven hours overboard trying to get Capt. [Edward] Bra Saunders' fishing boat off a bank where she had gone with us in a N.W. gale." Hemingway's recipe in the book offers these instructions: "Pour 1 jigger of absinthe into a champagne glass. Add iced champagne until it attains the proper opalescent milkiness. Drink 3 to 5 of these slowly."

For the present-day Death in the Afternoon, Deegan says it is essential to chill the absinthe before, as you don't want to add a chilled liquor, such as Champagne, to a room-temperature liquor, in this case, absinthe. Deegan considers Pernod Absinthe a classic ingredient with varying degrees of sweetness, and while he used Laurent-Perrier Brut Champagne, he said any dry champagne, doesn't have to be expensive, will work. He also recommends Death in the Afternoon as a good daytime cocktail. Hemingway would approve.

ABOUT BARREL PROOF: Barrel Proof was founded in 2014, distinguishing itself for its craft cocktails and its neighborhood feel. It is owned by LeBlanc + Smith.

ESPRIT DE CORPSE

SERVES 1

Courtesy Evan Hayes, Delachaise Wine and Cocktail Bar

3 ounces Brandy Sainte Louise

2 ounces St. Germain Elderflower Liqueur

1 ounce Aperol

3 ounces club soda, or 2 ounces club soda and 1 ounce ginger beer

Lemon peel

Add the first three ingredients into a large wine glass over ice. Then add the soda (or soda and ginger beer) and stir. Finish with a lemon peel.

* * *

According to Evan Hayes, owner of the Delachaise Wine and Cocktail Bar, the cognac is the aged "spirit," St. Germain adds some floral, "lively," notes, and Aperol adds some color with bite, which is then all balanced by the club soda or sweet ginger beer.

"It is a lighter riff on the Corpse Reviver which calls for absinthe," says Hayes. "It is lighter for hot New Orleans summers."

ABOUT THE DELACHAISE WINE AND COCKTAIL BAR: This neighborhood wine bar and bistro is located on New Orleans's historic St. Charles Avenue. It has been honored with being named "Best Date Place" and "Best Wine Bar" since it was founded in 2003.

KILL DEVIL COCKTAIL

SERVES 1

Courtesy Eric Solis, Columns

2 ounces Cheramie Rum (blanc)

½ ounce green Chartreuse

¼ ounce demerara syrup

2–3 dashes Angostura bitters

Dehydrated lime wheel, garnish

Combine all ingredients except lime wheel in mixing glass with ice cubes. Stir. Serve in a coupe glass and garnish with a dehydrated lime wheel.

* * *

"This cocktail caught my eye because I love all the ingredients that go in it!" says Eric Solis. The original recipe calls for rhum agricole, but Solis decided to substitute a New Orleans brand, Cheramie. According to Solis, Cheramie is an agricole-style rum that has a lot of the characteristics of a classic agricole but with the terroir of Louisiana.

"That, mixed with the green Chartreuse, a little sugar, and a few dashes of Angostura makes this stiff competition for the morbid!" he says, adding, "If you really want to put on a show, add a few drops of Wray and Nephew high-proof rum on top of a dehydrated lime wheel and light it on fire."

ABOUT COLUMNS: Columns is beloved by generations of New Orleanians, as well as those visiting the city. Built in 1883, the Thomas Sully–designed house has seen a variety of incarnations through the years from a family home to a boardinghouse, and then a hotel, which it is still today. Its bar is legendary for cocktails, and many like to imbibe on the large front porch—highlighted by Doric-style columns—and watch the St. Charles Avenue streetcar go by; others enjoy sitting in the bar with its impressive architectural details.

THE RESURRECTION

SERVES 1

Courtesy Southern Food and Beverage Museum/Museum of the American Cocktail

1 hibiscus flower in syrup

2 ounces Facundo Neo Silver Rum

1 part lime juice

1 part Sorel hibiscus liqueur

1 part Toulouse Rouge Absinthe (absinthe rouge)

Place 1 hibiscus flower in a chilled rocks glass. In a shaker full of ice add the rum, lime juice, liqueur, and absinthe. Stir until the mixture is chilled. Strain into the prepared glass and begin "the resurrection."

* * *

"My personal favorite absinthe drink. Very boozy and a bit irreverent," says Liz Williams, founder of the National Food & Beverage Foundation and the Southern Food & Beverage Museum.

The bar at the museum is built around the actual physical bar from Bruning's Restaurant, which opened in 1859 offshore in Lake Pontchartrain. The restaurant was destroyed during Hurricane Katrina. Descendants of the Bruning family donated it to the museum, whose staff restored it and placed it in the museum at 1504 Oretha Castle Haley Boulevard, New Orleans. Patrons of the museum are invited to have a drink as they explore the museum filled with culinary and cocktail treasures from the American South and the world.

VAMPIRE'S KISS

SERVES 1

Courtesy Bar Epilogue, the Chicory House

2 ounces Maker's Mark
1 ounce Fruitful fig liqueur
1 ounce tart cherry juice
Lemon twist

Add ingredients to a mixing glass with ice, stir until chilled, strain and serve in a rocks glass with a large ice cube. Garnish with a lemon twist.

ABOUT BAR EPILOGUE, THE CHICORY HOUSE: Bar Epilogue is located at the Garden District Book Shop in The Rink. Co-owner Barkley Rafferty and the Garden District Bookshop's Zach Hunt were inspired by author and New Orleans native Anne Rice, who lived and worked in the Garden District, which she also used as inspiration for her novels.

"The Garden District Book Shop was the home bookstore for Anne for many years, and we are honoring her legacy here in New Orleans and the many visitors who come to New Orleans because of her writing," says Rafferty.

Rafferty and Hunt pulled out everything red that was stocking the bar. Why red? It represented blood—as in vampires, the focus of many of Rice's books, including *Interview with the Vampire.* After three test runs, they found the perfect combination.

ZOMBIE

SERVES 1

Courtesy Jessica B. Harris

1 ounce white rum, such as Bacardi Light

1 ounce amber rum, such as Appleton Estate Special Gold

1 ounce dark rum, such as Mount Gay

½ ounce maraschino liqueur

1 ounce pineapple juice

1 ounce freshly squeezed strained lime juice

1 ounce freshly squeezed strained lemon juice

1 ounce passion fruit syrup

Crushed ice

151-proof dark rum, such as Bacardi

1 wedge pineapple for garnish

1 sprig fresh mint for garnish

Combine all of the ingredients except the 151 rum and garnishes in a cocktail shaker with a scoop of crushed ice. Shake vigorously and strain into a highball glass. Float a spoonful of 151 rum on top by slowly pouring it over the back of a spoon into the glass. Garnish with pineapple wedge, mint sprig and a straw. Serve immediately.

* * *

The Zombie is a "tiki" drink that was originally created by New Orleans-born Ernest Raymond Beaumont Gannt, aka Donn Beach, who in 1933 started the famous Hollywood restaurant Don the Beachcomber, which became the center of "tiki" culture. This Zombie recipe is a variation of the one he created in 1934, which was not set on fire like some other versions. Rumor has it the drink was created for a hungover customer, who returned days later to say he felt like he had been turned into a "zombie."

This recipe is from *Rum Drinks: 50 Caribbean Cocktails, from Cuba Libre to Rum Daisy* [2009], by Jessica B. Harris, a culinary historian, professor, journalist, and the author of fifteen cookbooks. Her book *High on the Hog: A Culinary Journey from Africa to America* was adapted in 2021 into a four-part Netflix series. She won a James Beard Foundation Lifetime Achievement Award in 2020.

The Obituary Cocktail, photographed at Cure. Photo by Chris Granger.

RESOURCES

BOOKS, BARS, DISTILLERIES, AND MORE

BARS/DISTILLERIES

Atelier Vie (distillery), 3928 Euphrosine St. ateliervie.com.

Bar Epilogue, the Chicory House, Garden District Book Shop at The Rink, 2727 Prytania St. gardendistrictbookshop.com.

Barrel Proof, 1201 Magazine St. drinkbarrelproof.com.

Cafe Lafitte in Exile (Lafitte's), 901 Bourbon St. lafittes.com.

Columns, 3811 St. Charles Ave. thecolumns.com.

Cure, 4905 Freret St. curenola.com.

Delachaise Wine Bar & Bistro, 3442 St. Charles Ave. thedelechaise.com.

Fives, 529 St. Ann St. (Pontalba Building, Jackson Square). fives.bar.

Gilded Perch, ParkView Historic Hotel, 7004 St. Charles Ave. parkview guesthouse.com.

Jewel of the South, 1026 St. Louis St. jewelnola.com.

Lafitte's Blacksmith Shop, 941 Bourbon St. lafittesblacksmithshop.com.

Lula Distillery, 1532 St. Charles Ave. lulanola.com.

Old Alker Distillery, 8304 Oak St. oldalkerdistillery.com.

Porchjam Distillery, 3918 Gravier St. porch-jame.com.

Seven Three Distilling Co., 301 N. Claiborne Ave. seventhreedistilling.com.

The Sazerac House, 101 Magazine St. sazerachouse.com.

Southern Food & Beverage Museum/The Museum of American Cocktail, 1504 Oretha Castle Haley Blvd. southernfood.org.

RADIO

Joe Frank radio program, "Home," featuring Grace Zabriskie. Originally aired on KCRW, Santa Monica public radio. joefrank.com.

PODCAST

NOLADrinks Show with Bryan Dias. noladrinks.com.

BOOKS

Arthur, Stanley Clisby. *Famous New Orleans Drinks and How to Mix 'Em.* New Orleans: Harmanson, 1937.

Baird, Sarah. *New Orleans Cocktails: An Elegant Collection of over 100 Recipes Inspired by the Big Easy.* Nashville: Cider Mill, 2017.

Barnett, Richard. *The Book of Gin.* New York: Grove, 2011.

Berry, Jason. *City of a Million Dreams: A History of New Orleans at Year 300.* Chapel Hill: University of North Carolina Press, 2018.

Bodenheimer, Neal. *Cure: New Orleans Drinks and How to Mix 'Em from the Award-Winning Bar.* New York: Abrams, 2022.

Breaux, T. A., and Betina J. Wittels. *Absinthe: The Exquisite Elixir.* Chicago: Chicago Review Press, 2017.

Celestan, Karen, and Eric Waters. *Freedom's Dance: Social Aid and Pleasure Clubs in New Orleans.* Baton Rouge: LSU Press, 2018.

Collier, Phillip. *Making New Orleans: Products Past and Present.* New Orleans: Philbeau, 2013.

Collier, Phillip, and Jennifer Adams. *Phillip Collier's Mixing New Orleans: Cocktails and Legends.* New Orleans: Philbeau, 2007.

Davis, William C. *The Pirates Lafitte: The Treacherous World of the Corsairs of the Gulf.* Boston: Mariner, 2006.

DeMers, John. *The Vieux Carré.* Baton Rouge: LSU Press, 2023.

English, Camper. *Doctors and Distillers: The Remarkable Medicinal History of Beer, Wine, Spirits and Cocktails.* New York: Penguin, 2022.

Gerber, Cheryl. *The Danse Macabre: Celebration and Survival in New Orleans.* Baton Rouge: LSU Press, 2024.

Hamilton, John Marshall. *The French 75.* Baton Rouge: LSU Press, 2024.

Hammond, Hilda Phelps, and Olive Leonhardt. *Shaking Up Prohibition in New Orleans: Authentic Vintage Cocktails from A to Z.* Baton Rouge: LSU Press, 2015.

Harris, Jessica B. *Rum Drinks: 50 Caribbean Cocktails, from Cuba Libre to Rum Daisy.* San Francisco: Chronicle, 2009.

Held, John, Jr. *Peychaud's New Orleans Cocktails.* New Orleans: A. M. & J. Solari, 1935. Available online at euvs-vintage-cocktail-books.cld.bz/1935-Peychaud-s-New-Orleans-Cocktails/1.

Kinney, Robert. *The Bachelor in New Orleans.* New Orleans: Borman House, 1942.

McCaffety, Kerri. *Obituary Cocktail: The Great Saloons of New Orleans.* New Orleans: Pontalba Press, 1998.

McNally, Tim. *The Sazerac.* Baton Rouge: LSU Press, 2020.

Moss, Robert F. *The Roffignac.* Baton Rouge: LSU Press, 2024.

North, Sterling, and Carl Kroch, eds. *So Red the Nose; or, Breath in the Afternoon, Cocktail Recipes by 30 Leading Authors.* New York: Farrar & Rinehart, 1935.

Perez, Frank, and Jeffrey Palmquist. *In Exile: The History and Lore Surrounding New Orleans Gay Culture and Its Oldest Gay Bar.* London: LL Publications, 2012.

Reed, John Shelton. *Dixie Bohemia: A French Quarter Circle in the 1920s.* Baton Rouge: LSU Press, 2012.

Songy, Marielle. *The Absinthe Frappé.* Baton Rouge: LSU Press, 2023.

Strachan, Sue. *The Café Brûlot.* Baton Rouge: LSU Press, 2021.

Stuart, Thos. *Stuart's Fancy Drinks and How to Mix Em.* New York: Excelsior, 1904. Available online at euvs-vintage-cocktail-books.cld.bz/1904-Stuart-s-Fancy-Drinks-and-How-To-Mix-Them.

Thomas, Jerry. *Jerry Thomas Bartenders Guide, 1887 Reprint.* Chump Change, 1887.

Tichi, Cecelia. *Jazz Age Cocktails: History, Lore, and Recipes from America's Roaring Twenties.* New York: New York University Press, 2021.

Touchet, Leo. *Rejoice When You Die: The New Orleans Jazz Funerals.* Baton Rouge: LSU Press, 1998.

Turner, Richard Brent. *Jazz Religion, the Second Line and Black New Orleans.* Bloomington: Indiana University Press, 2009.

Vogt, Lloyd. *Historic Buildings of the French Quarter.* New Orleans: Pelican, 2002.

Widmer, Mary Lou. *New Orleans in the Forties.* New Orleans: Pelican, 2007.

———. *New Orleans in the Thirties.* New Orleans: Pelican, 1991.

Williams, Elizabeth, and Chris McMillian. *Lift Your Spirits: A Celebratory History of Cocktail Culture in New Orleans.* Baton Rouge: LSU Press, 2016.

Wohl, Kit. *New Orleans Classic Cocktails.* New Orleans: Pelican, 2012.

Wondrich, Davis. *Imbibe! From Absinthe Cocktail to Whiskey Smash, A Salute in Stories and Drinks to "Professor" Professor Jerry Thomas, Pioneer of the American Bar.* 2007. Rev. ed. New York: Penguin 2015.

PRINT AND ONLINE ARTICLES

ABSINTHE

"Absinthe Tale." *La Fée.* lafee.com/history-of-absinthe.

"Distillerie Henri-Louis Pernod (Caves Byrrh)." *Difford's Guide.* diffords guide.com/producers/291/distillerie-henri-louis-pernod-caves-byrrh /history.

Hendrickson, Jay B. New Orleans Absinthe History. neworleansabsinthe-history.com.

Keller, Matt. "The Swisstory of Absinthe." *Trink Magazine,* April 7, 2021. trinkmag.com/articles/the-swisstory-of-absinthe/.

Simon, Lucy. "Absinthe Explained: Everything You Want to Know." Food andwine.com, updated December 9, 2022. foodandwine.com/cocktails -spirits/what-is-absinthe.

"Val-de-Travers: The Birthplace of Absinthe." *La Clandestine.* laclandestine .com/en/laclandestine/the-birthplace.

GIN, MARTINIS

Archibald, Anna. "Everything You Need to Know about Old Tom Gin." Liquor.com, updated December 5, 2020. liquor.com/articles/what-is -old-tom-gin.

Coats, Geraldine. "The First Record of the Word 'Gin.'" Gintime. gintime .com/features/the-first-record-of-the-word-gin/.

Dingwell, Kate. "What Is London Dry Gin?" *Food & Wine,* March 20, 2024. foodandwine.com/what-is-london-dry-gin-8611810.

"Essential Terminology: How to Order the Perfect Martini." *The Sipsmith Blog,* November 25, 2021. sipsmith.com/us/essential-martini-terminology-ordering-the-perfect-martini/.

Figes, Lydia. "The Gin Craze: How William Hogarth Captured the Spirit of Georgian Britain." *Art UK,* November 9, 2020. artuk.org/discover/stories/the-gin-craze-how-william-hogarth-captured-the-spirit-of-georgian-britain.

Gray, Kevin. "Martinez." Liquor.com, updated March 7, 2023. liquor.com/recipes/martinez.

"Jenever (Genever)." *I Am Expat.* iamexpat.nl/lifestyle/dutch-food.

"Juniper." Britannica. britannica.com/plant/juniper.

"Martini History." *Difford's Guide.* diffordsguide.com/g/1121/martini/martini-history.

Meehan, Jim. "Manhattan Cocktail." *Food & Wine,* updated August 10, 2023. foodandwine.com/recipes/manhattan-cocktails-2009.

Morgan, Audrey. "The Right Way to Order a Martini." Liquor.com, March 9, 2023. liquor.com/best-martini-guide-7253539.

"Plymouth Gin." The Gin Guild. theginguild.com/ginopedia/gin-brands/plymouth-gin/.

"Plymouth Gin." Pernod Ricard. pernod-ricard.com/en/brands/plymouth-gin.

"Sloe Gin Fizz. Liquor.com, updated Nov. 3, 2020. liquor.com/recipes/sloe-gin-fizz.

"Why Was Gin Nicknamed 'Mother's Ruin'? *Spirit of Harrogate.* spiritofharrogate.co.uk/blogs/news/why-was-gin-nicknamed-mother-s-ruin.

Whymark, Bethany. "The A–Z of Gin: O is for . . . Old Tom," *Gin Magazine,* August 1, 2022, gin-mag.com/2022/08/01/the-a-z-of-gin-old-tom-gin-historical-styles

VERMOUTH

Dingwall, Kate. "The 8 Best Vermouths for a Martini, According to Bartenders." Liquor.com, November 27, 2023. Liquor.com, liquor.com/best-vermouth-martini-8406941.

Newman, Kara. "Understanding the Main Types of Vermouth." Liquor.com, March 27, 2023, liquor.com/vermouth-types-explainer-7371802.

"Vermouth, The Refreshing Appetite Stimulator," Drymartiniorg.com, drymartiniorg.com/historia-origenes-vermut.

BAR HISTORY

Mullener, Elizabeth. "The Queen of Cuisine: Ella Brennan Regarded as One of the Most Revolutionary Restaurateurs in World." *Times-Picayune,* October 8, 2007. nola.com/entertainment_life/eat-drink/the-queen-of-cuisine-ella-brennan-regarded-as-one-of-most-revolutionary-restaurateurs-in-world/article.

O'Neill, Molly. "Stirring the Pot With: Ella Brennan; In a Restaurant Family, Big Mama's the Boss." *New York Times,* July 29, 1992. nytimes.com/1992/07/29/garden/stirring-the-pot-with-ella-brennan-in-a-restaurant-family-big-mama-s-the-boss.html.

Perez, Frank. "Tom Caplinger and How Lafitte's Went into Exile." *Ambush Magazine,* March 6, 2024. ambushmag.com/tom-caplinger-and-how-lafittes-went-into-exile/.

Scott, Mike. "Digging for Truth: The Real Story of Lafitte's Blacksmith Shop in the French Quarter: What's Fact, What's Fiction." NOLA.com, January 29, 2024. nola.com/entertainment_life/home_garden/lafittes-blacksmith-shop-intrigues-even-without-the-fiction/article.

DEATH IN NEW ORLEANS

"Ancient Choctaw Burial Practice." "Iti Fabvssa," *Biskinik,* February 2012. choctawnationculture.com/media.

Bartels, Matthew Duane. "Top Ten Unique Facts about Burial Practices in New Orleans." ListVerse, March 5, 2023. listverse.com/2023/03/05/top-ten-unique-facts-about-burial-practices-in-new-orleans/.

Campanella, Richard. "Pauger's Savvy Move." *Preservation in Print,* May 2014, richcampanella.com/wp-content/uploads/2020/02/article_Campanella_Preservation-in-Print_2014_May_Pauger-Savvy-Move.pdf.

"Choctaws Have Long History of Remembering and Honoring Loved Ones." "Iti Fabvssa," *Biskinik,* November 1, 2020. choctawnation.com/biskinik/iti-fabvssa/choctaws-have-long-history-of-remembering-and-honoring-loved-ones/.

Darensbourg, Jeffery. "Bulbnacha." 64 Parishes. 64parishes.org/entry/bulbancha.

"Day of the Dead." history.com/topics/halloween/day-of-the-dead.

"Jean-Baptiste Le Moyne de Bienviille." American Battlefield Trust. battlefields.org/learn/biographies/jean-baptiste-le-moyne-de-bienville.

King, Matt. "A History of the French Quarter." *French Quarter Citizens,* October 23, 2011. frenchquartercitizens.org/a-history-of-the-french-quarter.

Magill, John. "History of French Quarter." French Quarter Management District. fqmd.org/history-of-french-quarter/.

Neidenbach, Elizabeth Clark. "Cholera in Louisiana." 64parishes.org/entry/cholera-in-louisiana.

Perkins, Emily, and John Magill. "In the Late 1800s, Devastating Yellow Fever Epidemics Forced New Orleans to Confront Its Sanitation Problem." hnoc.org/publications/first-draft/late-1800s-devastating-yellow-fever-epidemics-forced-new-orleans-confront.

Rhodes, Kalie. "The Native Roots of the French Market." New Orleans Historical. neworleanshistorical.org/items/show/1641.

MUSEUMS OF CULINARY AND COCKTAIL HISTORY IN NEW ORLEANS

Historic New Orleans Collection, 520 and 533 Royal St. hnoc.org.

Louisiana State Museum. louisianastatemuseum.org.

New Orleans Museum of Art, 1 Collins C. Diboll Circle. noma.org.

New Orleans Pharmacy Museum, 514 Chartres St. pharmacymuseum.org.

The Sazerac House, 101 Magazine St. sazerachouse.com.

Southern Food & Beverage Museum/The Museum of the American Cocktail, 1504 Oretha Castle Haley Blvd. southernfood.org. The museum has an amazing display of absinthe ephemera.

Southern Food & Beverage Resource Center/Boyd Hospitality and Culinary Library, Nunez Community College Library, 3710 Paris Rd., Chalmette. southernfood.org/research-center.

Tulane University Special Collections (includes the Hogan Archive of New Orleans Music and New Orleans Jazz, the Louisiana Research Collection, Rare Books, the Southeastern Architectural Archive, and University Archives). library.tulane.edu/tusc.

Williams Research Center (part of Historic New Orleans Collection), 410 Chartres St. hnoc.org.

ICONIC NEW ORLEANS COCKTAILS

The Sazerac

The Café Brûlot

The Vieux Carré

The Absinthe Frappé

The French 75

The Roffignac

The Brandy Milk Punch

The Ramos Gin Fizz

The Obituary Cocktail